An easy guide to factor analysis

D0162350

Factor analysis is a statistical technique widely used in psychology and the social sciences. With the advent of powerful computers, factor analysis and other multivariate methods are now available to many more people. *An Easy Guide to Factor Analysis* presents and explains factor analysis as clearly and simply as possible. The author, Paul Kline, carefully defines all statistical terms and demonstrates step-by-step how to work out a simple example of principal components analysis and rotation. He further explains other methods of factor analysis, including confirmatory and path analysis, and concludes with a discussion of the use of the technique with various examples.

An Easy Guide to Factor Analysis is the clearest, most coherent introduction to factor analysis for students. All those who need to use statistics in psychology and the social sciences will find it invaluable.

Paul Kline is Professor of Psychometrics at the University of Exeter. He has been using and teaching factor analysis for thirty years. His previous books include *Intelligence: The Psychometric View* (Routledge 1990) and *The Handbook of Psychological Testing* (Routledge 1992).

Other titles by Paul Kline available from ROUTLEDGE

An easy guide to factor analysis

Paul Kline

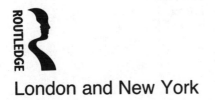

London and New York

First published 1994
by Routledge
11 New Fetter Lane, London EC4P 4EE

Simultaneously published in the USA and Canada
by Routledge
29 West 35th Street, New York, NY 10001

Table 10.1 and Figure 10.1 are from R. D. Goffin and D. N. Jackson (1988) 'The structural validity of the Index of Organizational Reactions', *Multivariate Behavioural Research* 23: 327–47. Figures 10.2 and 10.3 are from R. H. Hoyle and R. D. Lennox (1991) 'Latent structure of self-monitoring', *Multivariate Behavioural Research* 26: 511–40. All reproduced by permission of Lawrence Erlbaum Associates, Inc., New Jersey.

Typeset in Bembo by Florencetype Ltd, Kewstoke, Avon

Printed and bound in Great Britain by
TJ Press (Padstow) Ltd, Padstow, Cornwall

British Library Cataloguing in Publication Data
A catalogue record for this book is available from the British Library.

Library of Congress Cataloging in Publication Data
Kline, Paul.
  An easy guide to factor analysis / Paul Kline.
    p.   cm.
  Includes bibliographical references and index.
  1. Factor analysis.   2. Psychology–Statistical methods.
  3. Social sciences–Statistical methods.   I. Title.
BF93.2.F32K55 1993
519.5'354–dc20
                                                              93-3482
                                                              CIP

ISBN 0-415-09489-5 (hbk)
ISBN 0-415-09490-9 (pbk)

Contents

Illustrations

Chapter 1

A general description of factor analysis

AIMS OF THE BOOK

Factor analysis is a statistical technique widely used in psychology and the social sciences. Indeed in some branches of psychology, especially those in which tests or questionnaires have been administered, it is a necessity. With the advent of powerful computers and the dreaded statistical packages which go with them factor analysis and other multivariate methods are available to those who have never been trained to understand them. I have examined countless theses in which the factor analytic results were simply a source of fear and confusion to the students who were praying that they would not be asked to explain them.

Furthermore, I am regularly approached by colleagues not only in my own university but in other departments of psychology and education, especially, for advice on interpreting and carrying out factor analyses. None of these colleagues and students is stupid. There are several reasons why they have failed to understand factor analysis. First, in Great Britain, at least among social scientists there is a general fear of mathematics. Equations freeze the mind, rendering it blank. Second, in many departments of psychology and education factor analysis is not well taught, or not taught at all, as I have found in teaching postgraduates. As in my time as a postgraduate, students are referred to a number of 'excellent books, which tell you all you need to know'.

Regrettably, it is precisely these books which are the source of the problem. First let it be said that there are a number of excellent books on factor analysis and later in this *Easy Guide* I shall refer to them. However, except to mathematicians and those who have a reasonable knowledge and insight into factor analysis, they are unreadable and close to incomprehensible. Indeed only one book, to this writer's knowledge, has ever attempted to simplify factor analysis to a level which students might be expected to understand – Dennis Child's *The Essentials of Factor Analysis* (latest edition 1990). Even this book many students find too hard and some important aspects of the technique are not included. Why these books are so difficult stems from the fact that they are usually written by good mathematicians. These find mathematical arguments and the equivalence of apparently completely different formulae so obvious as to require no explanation.

The aim of the *Easy Guide* is to provide an explication of the basic mathematics of factor analysis which anybody who can manage any form of tertiary education can follow, so that, at the end of the book, readers will understand factor analysis. All mathematical terms, even the most simple, will be explained. All mathematical processes will be illustrated by examples. Readers will not be expected to make mathematical inferences. Each step will be explained. If the basic mathematics of factor analysis is understood, readers will then be able to use the technique effectively for research and, perhaps more importantly, they will be able to evaluate its use in journal papers. For much factor analytic research, as has been shown by Cattell (1978), is technically inadequate, rendering the results valueless. In addition I believe that, after reading this book, the excellent books to which I have already referred will become the useful texts which they were intended to be.

Finally I should like to say that the desire to write this book derived from my own personal experiences in working with factor analysis over almost thirty years. I came into psychology with no mathematical background and would have been entirely defeated by factor analysis had I not had the good fortune to work with Professor Warburton of Manchester University, who had the patience to explain what I could not understand without that contempt for one's stupidity which all too often accompanies mathematical or statistical explanation. I hope that the *Easy Guide* will provide just such an explication.

GENERAL DESCRIPTION OF FACTOR ANALYSIS

I shall begin with a general, verbal description of factor analysis, describing the aims and logic of the method, the kinds of questions it can answer, and its different varieties. I shall do this because I have found that the mathematical procedures become more comprehensible if the purpose and nature of factor analysis is already known.

What is factor analysis? Factor analysis consists of a number of statistical techniques the aim of which is to simplify complex sets of data. In the social sciences factor analysis is usually applied to correlations between variables and these must now be described.

Definition of a correlation coefficient   A correlation is a numerical measure of the degree of agreement between two sets of scores. It runs from +1 to −1: +1 indicates full agreement, 0 no relationship and −1 complete disagreement.

Suppose we have two sets of scores in English and maths (Table 1.1).

Table 1.1 Scores in English and maths

Subjects	English	Maths
1	100	100
2	95	95
3	91	91
.	.	.
.	.	.
.	.	.
N	0	0

In this example (which would be virtually impossible in real life), in which the scores of N subjects (note that N describes the size of a sample) on English and maths are set out, it is evident that there is perfect agreement. In this case the correlation would be +1. If the opposite had occurred and the top person in English had been the bottom in maths and the second person in English had been second from bottom in maths and so on through the list the correlation would have been −1.

Notice that with correlations of ±1 perfect predictions from one score to the other can be made. That is one of the important features of correlations in the social sciences: they enable prediction from one set of scores to another, although in real life correlations are almost never equal to ±1. The closer they get to 1 (regardless of sign) the higher the degree of agreement between the scores and thus the better the possible prediction. If correlations are squared the percentage agreement of the sets of scores is indicated.

Thus a correlation of 0.8 indicates 64 per cent agreement and 0.2 shows only 4 per cent agreement (0.2 squared is 0.04, not 0.4). A correlation of 0 indicates that there is no relationship at all between the two sets of scores.

Definition of a correlation matrix   A correlation matrix is a set of correlation coefficients between a number of variables.

Thus if we have five variables the correlation matrix will be of the kind shown in Table 1.2. The following points should be noted about this correlation matrix.

Table 1.2 A correlation matrix

Variable	Variable				
	1	2	3	4	5
1	1.0	0.31	0.40	0.24	0.35
2	0.31	1.0	0.53	0.12	0.04
3	0.40	0.53	1.0	0.01	0.42
4	0.24	0.12	0.01	1.0	0.25
5	0.35	0.04	0.42	0.25	1.0

1 Each variable is assumed to correlate perfectly with itself. In practice, which will be discussed in later chapters of this book, this is not always the case. What goes into the diagonals of the correlation matrix is important in understanding and interpreting factor analyses.
2 There is considerable redundancy in the matrix, each entry appearing twice, as it logically must.
3 Factor analysis is designed to simplify these correlation matrices. With as few as five variables there are 25 entries – which are hard enough to keep in one's head. In a large study with perhaps 100 variables there are 10,000 correlations. Without some simplifying procedure such a matrix would be incomprehensible.
4 In a large matrix of correlations, it is reasonable to ask what might account for the correlations. An example will clarify the point. Suppose that we have administered 100 different tests of ability and school attainment. In fact, the resulting correlation matrix would consist of positive and often high correlations in the region of 0.5 and 0.6. A factor analysis would reveal that

these could be accounted for by a small number of factors: intelligence, verbal ability and spatial ability. Thus instead of having to look at the scores on a 100 tests to understand these correlations, which no human being is able to do, we could understand them in terms of three scores – on intelligence, verbal ability and spatial ability.

The example in (4) asserts and illustrates that factor analysis can simplify a matrix of correlations, but it is not meaningful without further explanation and this is set out below.

Definition of a factor   As Royce (1963) has demonstrated, whilst there have been many different definitions of a factor there is a common underlying trend to them all. Essentially a factor is a dimension or construct which is a condensed statement of the relationships between a set of variables. This has been more precisely refined by Royce (1963), who states that a factor is *a construct operationally defined by its factor loadings*.

This is an excellent definition although obviously factor loadings need to be defined.

Definition of factor loadings   Factor loadings are the correlations of a variable with a factor.

Table 1.3 Illustration of a factor analysis

Variables	Factor 1	Factor 2	Factor 3
Intelligence	0.82	0.63	0.44
Non-verbal IQ	0.78	0.35	0.51
Vocabulary	0.68	0.64	0.21
Rhyming	0.28	0.59	0.18
Algebra	0.45	0.20	0.38
Geometry	0.50	0.17	0.69
Physics	0.41	0.13	0.37
Latin	0.58	0.70	0.20
French	0.32	0.68	0.17
History	0.25	0.43	0.12
Engineering	0.49	0.09	0.60

An artificial illustration will clarify this definition. Suppose that we have computed the factor analysis of a set of ability and attainment tests. At this point how this is done (which will be fully explained in later chapters of this book) does not matter. The factor analysis might well look like the analysis set out in Table 1.3. This example shows three factors in a typical factor analysis of abilities. There would be other factors but these illustrate the nature of factors and factor loadings extremely well.

The interpretation and meaning of factors

1 The results of a factor analysis simply set out a number of factors, as shown above. The meaning of these factors has to be deduced from the factor loadings – the coefficients set out in Table 1.3. The factor loadings are what are computed in the factor analysis. It must be stressed, however, that all interpretations of factors, based on loadings, should be validated against external criteria. Thus if we think we have an intelligence factor we might investigate whether high scorers showed other signs of intelligence, e.g. held good jobs or were highly successful at exams and so on.

2 The factor loadings are correlations of the variables with the factors. It is usual to regard factor loadings as high if they are greater than 0.6 (the positive or negative sign is irrelevant) and moderately high if they are above 0.3. Other loadings can be ignored. A more precise account of the significance and importance of factor loadings will be given later. From these loadings the following three deductions can be made.

3 Factor 1 correlates with all the school subjects but most highly with the intelligence tests. (Actually the technical term is loads rather than correlates and I shall use this from now on in the text.) This suggests that this is a general ability, which is important in all these tests. Since intelligence is usually defined as a general reasoning ability, it appears that this first factor should be identified from its loadings as general intelligence. Note that some school subjects load more highly on this factor than others – suggesting that intelligence is not so important for some subjects. History, in this example, appears not to require as much intelligence as Latin or geometry. Although this is an artificial example there is some evidence for such a difference (see Kline 1991).

4 Factor 2, by the same process of deduction as used above, must be verbal ability, as it loads highly on all those tests and subjects which involve language but rather low on other tests.

5 Factor 3 loads highly on intelligence and on geometry and engi-

neering. Both of the latter subjects require an ability to orient things in space and this suggests that this factor is spatial ability.

These five points, taken from the artificial example given in Table 1.3, illustrate clearly the nature of factors as constructs or dimensions defined by their loadings. They also illustrate how a complex set of data, in this instance a large number of scores on different tests, can be reduced and simplified. Thus if we wished to predict how well a subject would perform in these subjects in the future we could do so from scores on these three factors. We would not need to know all the test scores.

This, therefore, is the rationale of specifying factors as constructs or dimensions defined by their factor loadings. Given this definition I shall now discuss the utility of factor analysis in the social sciences, its aims and its logic.

THE UTILITY OF FACTOR ANALYSIS

Given, then, that factor analysis can be used to simplify correlation matrices, an important question still remains: what can be done with it and how can it be useful in the social sciences?

To answer this, one further point needs to be made about factor analysis. In the application of this method a distinction needs to be drawn between exploratory and confirmatory factor analysis.

Exploratory factor analysis: an illustration

In exploratory analysis the aim is to explore the field, to discover the main constructs or dimensions. It was for this purpose that factor analysis was originally developed by Spearman (1904), in the area of human abilities. He attempted to answer the question of why it was that human abilities are always positively correlated, what is referred to in the factor analysis of abilities as the positive manifold, i.e. all the correlations in the correlation matrix are positive.

From our description and interpretation of the factor analysis given in Table 1.3 it is clear how factor analysis can be used to answer this question. Rephrased in factor analytic terms the question becomes: what constructs or dimensions could account for the correlations between abilities? It was from this early work that the notion of general intelligence was developed – as factor analysis revealed that a general factor, loading on all variables, was highly important in accounting for the correlations. More precise definitions of what is meant by 'account for' and 'highly important', when referring to factors, will be given in Chapters 3 and 4.

This first example illustrates clearly one of the main uses of factor analysis in the social sciences. When there is a highly complex field, as there almost always is in real–life human affairs, as distinct from laboratory studies of human beings where one variable may be manipulated at a time, factor analysis simplifies the field by indicating what the important variables are. Let us take the educational example again. Suppose that we had before us a huge matrix of correlations between abilities and skills and we tried, without factor analysis, to answer the question of why these are positively correlated. A huge number of possibilities come to mind:

1 some people are good at school work and clever and this accounts for the results (this, however, is not an explanation since it simply throws the original question back a further stage: what makes these people clever and others not clever?);
2 some might argue that social class is the determiner;
3 others may argue that it is the ability to concentrate;
4 another hypothesis suggests that it is quality of education.

These are four obvious hypotheses and the moderate correlations between social class, educational level and test scores make two of them possible. The notion of concentration is also appealing.

Exploratory factor analysis would answer the original question and thus implicitly refute or confirm these four hypotheses. In fact, as has been mentioned, a general ability factor can be shown to be important in accounting for these correlations. As in our example of Table 1.3, there would be a general factor loading on intelligence tests and school attainment measures. Social class loads only low on such a factor. This means that social class is implicated to some extent, but not much, in performance at school. We all know of dim aristocrats and brilliant people from poor backgrounds. Of course, the actual findings are not important. If social class were a powerful determinant of school performance it would load highly on the factor on which the attainment tests loaded.

If a measure of the ability to concentrate were to be included in the matrix of correlations, this again would load only moderately on school performance. It plays a part, of course, but it is not critical. This ability is probably itself in any case related to

intelligence. Actually a moment's thought would show that concentration could not be a major determinant of performance. If this
were the case there would be little variation in school performance
since concentration is needed for all tasks. Again actual results are
not what matters in this illustration of the utility of factor analysis.
If concentration were important it would load highly on the attainment test factor. Identical arguments apply to the final hypothesis
concerning quality of education. If this were influential it would
load on the attainment test factor. If it were not, it would not do
so.

From this example of attainment testing it is clear that exploratory factor analysis is a powerful tool in elucidating its important
determiners and associated variables. In general in exploratory
analysis the rule is to put in as many variables as possible and see
what loads on the relevant factor. If our interest is in achievement at
school we simply look for all the variables which load on the same
factor as the achievement measures. If our interest were more
specific, say science performance, then we would look for a factor
specific to that and see what variables loaded on it.

Further examples of exploratory factor analysis

These are all practical questions. Some psychometrists have used
factor analysis to examine more theoretical issues. Thus in the field
of human abilities the question has concerned the number of human
abilities and their structure. This has been convincingly answered
by factor analysis which shows that there are two intelligence
factors and three other smaller factors – the ability to visualize, a
speed factor and a factor of fluency, the ability to retrieve material
from memory, as has been fully discussed by Cattell (1971). Not
only is this of considerable theoretical interest, but the selection of
the most important factors is essential for further study of the area.
Thus when the important factors are known, environmental and
genetic influences can be investigated and other determinants of
their variation, thus building up a psychology of abilities.
Exploratory factor analysis is an essential first step in the investigation of complex areas of human psychology.

It must not be thought that factor analysis is only suitable for the
study of attainment and ability. It is widely used in the study of
personality. Thus an important question concerns what are the
most important personality variables. Exploratory factor analysis

has proved excellent for this purpose. As many measures as possible are administered to subjects and the results are factored. In fact there is a general consensus that there are five pervasive factors, as is fully discussed in my *Personality: The Psychometric View* (Kline 1993).

Another important use of factor analysis is in the construction of psychological tests. The logic of this procedure is simple. Any test, ideally, should measure only one variable. To ensure this a large number of possible items are administered to subjects and the correlations between the items are subjected to factor analysis. Items which load the general factor are selected for the test.

A final example will illustrate the power of exploratory factor analysis as a statistical method. In a small-scale study of occupational choice we factored occupational choice along with a number of personality and interest tests. We then looked at what variables loaded on the factors concerned with such choice. Thus it was found, for example, that introversion and intelligence went along with science as a preferred career (Parker and Kline 1993).

In summary, it can be seen that exploratory factor analysis is ideal where data are complex and it is uncertain what the most important variables in the field are. This is hardly surprising given our definition of factors as constructs or dimensions which account for the relationships between variables and which are defined by their factor loadings.

Confirmatory analysis

Originally factor analysis was simply an exploratory statistical method. Recently however it has become possible to test hypotheses using factor analysis, a method developed by Joreskog (1973) and called confirmatory analysis. In this method, based upon previous studies or on relevant theory, factor loadings for the variables are hypothesized. Confirmatory factor analysis then proceeds to fit these loadings in the target matrix, as it is called, as closely as possible. How good the fit is can also be measured. Since the scientific method, as it is generally conceived, e.g. by Popper (1959), involves testing hypotheses confirmatory analysis has become acceptable to psychologists who were previously resistant to exploratory methods.

Confirmatory analysis will be scrutinized carefully in Chapter 6, although a full mathematical coverage will be beyond the scope of this book. However, it is sufficient to say at this point that in the social sciences it is often so difficult to specify with any precision what the factor loadings should be that confirmatory analysis is not highly useful. However, if the target matrix is specified in a more general fashion, e.g. each variable being specified as a high, low or zero loading, then it is difficult to reject the hypothesized target matrix. All these problems and difficulties together with the advantages of confirmatory factor analysis will be discussed, as has been stated, in Chapter 6.

It can be seen from all these points and arguments that factor analysis is a powerful technique of investigation with wide application in the social sciences. Yet although it is much used (or more strictly misused, which is part of the reason for writing the *Easy Guide*) many researchers, for whom it would be valuable, do not employ it because of a number of objections to the method. These will be briefly mentioned now, although they are all easily dealt with, as will be shown in the relevant chapters of this book.

OBJECTIONS TO FACTOR ANALYSIS

1 The main objection to factor analysis is that there is an infinity of mathematically equivalent solutions. While this is true, it is also the case that psychometrists have developed powerful methods of choosing the right solution. All these methods are fully explicated in Chapter 5 of this book.

2 Factor analysts frequently disagree as to what are the most important factors in the field. This is especially so, for example, in personality. This is really a specific instance of the first objection as it appears in practice. Often, disparity of results is due to poor factor analytic methods which readers of the *Easy Guide* will learn to spot.

3 It is difficult to replicate factor analyses. Again this stems from the first basic objection, although with sound methodology it can be overcome.

4 It is sometimes said that with factor analysis you only get what you put in so that it is difficult to see how the method can be useful. This objection is based upon faulty logic. It is the case that if, for example, in a study of abilities no measures of musical ability were included, then no factor of musical ability could emerge. From this it follows that in exploratory analyses it is

essential to sample variables as widely as possible. However, it does not follow from this that in factor analysis you only get out what you put in.

In test construction some authors include items which are essentially paraphrases of each other. These certainly will load a factor and in this case the objection does indeed hold. Cattell (1978) calls these useless factors bloated specifics and how to eliminate and identify these factors will be discussed in Chapters 8 and 10. However, it does not follow that this is always the case. For example, if I were to factor simply a set of school examination results, including only school subjects, three factors or so would account for the correlations: the ones which we discussed above – intelligence, verbal ability and spatial ability. Although no specific measures of these factors had been included in the study they would emerge because, in fact, they do determine the relationships between measures of school achievement.

In brief, this objection is sometimes valid. However, generally this is not so and, ironically, one of the most attractive aspects of factor analysis as a statistical method is that it can reveal constructs which were previously unknown.

CONCLUDING REMARKS

So far in this chapter I have explained the purpose and function of factor analysis and have defined factors. However, this verbal explanation has to be accepted on trust. In the following chapters I shall explicate the surprisingly simple algebra of factor analysis in such a way that its ability to account for correlations, the status of factors as constructs, the definition of factors in terms of loadings and the need to validate factors against external criteria will become obvious. Thus the algebra in the *Easy Guide* will aid understanding. With the basics of factor analysis understood, readers who wish to do so will be able to tackle the more comprehensive texts to which reference will be made in the relevant chapters. These books describe some of the more mathematically sophisticated procedures of factor analysis.

SUMMARY

1 Factor analysis is defined generally as a method for simplifying complex sets of data.

2 Factor analysis is usually, in the social sciences, applied to correlation matrices.

3 A factor is defined as a construct or dimension which can account for the relationships (correlations) between variables.

4 Factor loadings are defined as the correlations between variables and factors.

5 The definition in (4) enables a more precise definition of factors as constructs defined by their factor loadings.

6 The meaning and interpretation of factors is derived from their loadings, although these meanings must be externally validated.

7 Examples of the use of factor analysis, both practical and theoretical, in the fields of ability and personality are given.

8 A distinction is drawn between exploratory analysis, the most common use of the technique, and confirmatory analysis in which hypotheses can be tested.

9 Some objections to factor analysis are briefly discussed.

10 The most important of these – the infinity of equivalent solutions – is answered.

11 The claim that from factor analysis no more than is put in can be taken out is also discussed and is found to hold only in a small number of instances.

Chapter 2

Statistical terms and concepts

In this chapter I shall explain and discuss all the statistical concepts and terms which are involved in the computation of factor analyses. In addition I shall explain the symbols used in the algebra of the technique. For ease of explanation I shall usually assume that scores are test scores although they could be the measures of any variable such as height or social class.

SYMBOLS

X refers to a score on any variable, e.g. an intelligence test.

x refers to a deviation score. If a person scores 10 on a test and the average score of his or her group is 15, then the deviation score is -5. Similarly a score of 21 in that group would yield a deviation score of $+6$. As will be seen these deviation scores play an important part in factor analytic computations.

N refers to the number of subjects in a sample.

Σ (capital sigma) means 'sum of'. Thus ΣX means add together all the Xs – the scores on a test or variable. Similarly Σx means add together all the deviation scores.

There are other symbols used in the computations of factor analysis but these refer to statistical terms and concepts and will be explicated as the terms arise in the text.

BASIC STATISTICAL TERMS

Mean

The mean is the average score of any group on a test. It is often of interest to compare the mean scores of different groups on a test, e.g. of boys and girls on a reading test. The mean, $\bar{X}$, is given by

$$\bar{X} = \frac{\Sigma X}{N} \tag{2.1}$$

where ΣX is the sum of all scores on the test and N is the number in the sample. This is a calculation which most people do at various times in everyday life. The scores are added up and divided by the number of subjects.

The mean indicates the average score of a group and is sometimes referred to in textbooks as a measure of central tendency. It tells us what the group on average is like. However, this is not informative on its own unless the spread or dispersion of the scores in the group is also known. An artificial and exaggerated example will make this point. Suppose that we have two groups, A and B, each of five subjects, who have taken an intelligence test, the scores of which are given in Table 2.1. Applying formula (2.1) in both

Table 2.1 Intelligence test scores

Group A	Group B
10	20
10	1
10	15
9	2
11	12

cases we can see that the means are identical, i.e. 10. However, the groups are quite different – the scores of subjects in group A in no case overlap the scores of subjects in group B. This difference lies in the dispersion or spread of the scores. In group A the spread is small, in group B it is far larger. Clearly, therefore, it is necessary to have a measure of the dispersion of the scores as well as the mean if the scores of a group are to be properly described. This is given by the standard deviation.

Standard deviation

The standard deviation is a measure of dispersion or variation among scores. It is symbolized by either SD or σ (lower case sigma) and is given by

$$\text{SD or } \sigma = \sqrt{\frac{\Sigma x^2}{N}}$$

(2.2)

where Σx^2 is the sum of the squared deviations and N is the number in the sample. The scores from groups A and B can be used to illustrate this calculation (Table 2.2).

Table 2.2 Standard deviations of intelligence test scores

Group A				Group B			
X	$\bar{X}$	x	x^2	X	$\bar{X}$	x	x^2
10	10	0	0	20	10	10	100
10	10	0	0	1	10	9	81
10	10	0	0	15	10	5	25
9	10	1	1	2	10	8	64
11	10	1	1	12	10	2	4
Σx^2			2				274

Applying formula (2.2) we obtain

Group A   SD $= \sqrt{(2/5)} = \sqrt{(0.4)} = 0.632$
Group B   SD $= \sqrt{(274/5)} = \sqrt{(54.8)} = 7.40$.

Standard deviations are expressed in the same units as the test. Thus if this is a test with possible scores ranging from 0 to 20, the standard deviation gives us a good indication of the dispersion or spread of scores. As is obvious from these two extreme and tiny samples, group A has a very small dispersion and group B a large one.

Standard or Z scores

Z scores are an important means of transforming scores which enter into many aspects of factor and correlational analysis. Whereas test scores (raw scores) from different tests are not comparable because, as is obvious, 50 in a test with a top score of 50 is quite different from the same score in a test where the maximum is

100, Z scores, on the other hand, are always comparable. The Z score is calculated using

$$Z = \frac{X - M}{\text{SD}}$$

(2.3)

where X is a raw score on a test, M is the mean of the group and SD is the standard deviation.

Since the arithmetic of our previous examples is awkward I shall illustrate formula (2.3) with easier examples.

Suppose that we have two tests, an English test and a maths test. The former has a mean of 100 and a standard deviation of 20, the latter a mean of 50 and a standard deviation of 10. The examples given in Table 2.3 indicate the nature of Z scores. They have means of 0 and standard deviations of 1. Their comparability is made clear in these examples. Thus 100 and 50 are equivalent on these two tests since they are both means and similarly 80 and 40 are equivalent because they are each one standard deviation below the mean.

Table 2.3 Examples of Z scores

English test	$(X - M)/$SD	Z score	Maths test	$(X - M)/$SD	Z score
100	$(100 - 100)/20$	0	63	$(63 - 50)/10$	+1.3
80	$(80 - 100)/20$	−1	50	$(50 - 50)/10$	0
120	$(120 - 100)/20$	+1	40	$(40 - 50)/10$	−1
130	$(130 - 100)/20$	+1.5	80	$(80 - 50)/10$	+3

From this it is clear that the mean and standard deviation are excellent descriptors of group scores and Z scores are highly useful where scores from different tests need to be compared.

Variance

Another measure of variation is the variance, which we have already encountered when computing the standard deviation. The variance is the standard deviation squared and is therefore given by

$$\text{Variance} = \frac{\Sigma x^2}{N}$$

(2.4)

where Σx^2 is the sum of the squared deviations and N is the number in the sample.

Thus the variance is the average of the squared deviations. The variance and the standard deviation are closely related. Generally, the standard deviation is used as a descriptive statistic and the variance is used in further statistical analysis because, as Nunnally (1978) points out, it is well suited to it. The variance is particularly important in factor analysis because, as will be shown in subsequent chapters, factors are able to account for or explain the variance in test scores.

Correlation

As was mentioned in the previous chapter the correlation is a measure of the degree of agreement between two sets of scores from the same individuals. Factor analysis is usually applied to matrices of correlations (see Chapter 1) in an attempt to simplify them. Before factor analysis can be understood it is essential that correlations be fully explained.

Although there are various different forms of correlation, for the purpose of the *Easy Guide* I shall restrict myself to the index of correlation which is most widely used – the Pearson product–moment correlation, developed by the great British statistician Pearson. Nunnally (1978) gives a clear explanation of why it is called a product–moment correlation, although at this juncture this explanation would serve only as a distraction. The Pearson correlation r is calculated using

$$r = \frac{\Sigma x_1 x_2}{(\Sigma x_1 \Sigma x_2)^{1/2}}$$

(2.5)

where x_1 is the deviation score on one test and x_2 is the corresponding deviation score on another test. In this formula, subscripts 1 and 2 refer to tests 1 and 2, as is usual with this type of statistics.

The top line of formula (2.5) consists of the sum of the cross product of two sets of deviation scores. When it is divided by N, the number of people taking the two tests, it becomes the covariance. This is also implicated in factor analyses. The covariance σ_{12} is calculated using

$$\sigma_{12} = \frac{\Sigma x_1 x_2}{N}$$

(2.6)

where x_1 and x_2 are defined as above.

Worked example of a correlation

Formula (2.5) will be clarified by a simple example which is given in Table 2.4 (p. 20). Applying formula (2.5) we obtain (for $N = 7$)

$$\frac{14}{\sqrt{(48)}\ \sqrt{(24)}} = \frac{14}{6.92 \times 4.89} = \frac{14}{33.90} = 0.413.$$

Thus the Pearson product–moment correlation between A and B is 0.413.

Normally, of course, in real-life data the mean is not a whole number so that working out the deviations in this way and squaring them becomes extremely tedious. However, it is possible to express this formula in various different ways and a raw score formula is given in most textbooks. I have used this example because by the use of the variance and covariance it indicates most clearly the nature of the product–moment correlation.

Correlations can be computed from raw scores as follows.

$$r = \frac{N\Sigma X_1 X_2 - \Sigma X_1 \Sigma X_2}{[N\Sigma X_1^2 - (\Sigma X_1)^2]^{1/2}\ [N\Sigma X_2^2 - (\Sigma X_2)^2]^{1/2}}. \qquad (2.7)$$

This equation is algebraically equivalent to formula (2.5). A worked example will clarify the terms in formula (2.7) and I shall use the same data as before (Table 2.5).

From formula (2.7)

$$r = \frac{7 \times 294 - 35 \times 56}{\sqrt{(7 \times 223)} - 35^2 \times \sqrt{(7 \times 472)} - 56^2}$$

$$= \frac{2,058 - 1,960}{\sqrt{(1,561)} - 1,225 \times \sqrt{(3,304)} - 3,136}$$

$$= \frac{98}{\sqrt{(336)} \times \sqrt{(168)}}$$

$$= \frac{98}{18.33 \times 12.96}$$

$$= \frac{98}{237.584}$$

thus, from formula (2.7),

$$r = 0.413.$$

Table 2.4 Data for worked example

Subject	Test A	Mean	x_1	x_1^2	Test B	Mean	x_2	x_2^2	$x_1 x_2$
1	3	5	−2	4	10	8	+2	4	−4
2	3	5	−2	4	9	8	+1	1	−2
3	5	5	0	0	8	8	0	0	0
4	7	5	+2	4	9	8	+1	1	+2
5	7	5	+2	4	7	8	−1	1	−2
6	9	5	+4	16	9	8	+1	1	+4
7	1	5	−4	16	4	8	−4	16	+16
Total				48				24	+14

Table 2.5 Computing correlations from raw scores

Subject	Test A	X^2	Test B	X^2	$X_1 X_2$
1	3	9	10	100	30
2	3	9	9	81	27
3	5	25	8	64	40
4	7	49	9	81	63
5	7	49	7	49	49
6	9	81	9	81	81
7	1	1	4	16	4
Total	35	223	56	472	294

A few points should be noted from these worked examples.

1 It is obvious how, in a small sample such as this, one single subject can hugely affect the result. If subject 7 had not been at the extreme on both tests, much the worst, the correlation would have been negligible. Thus to be reliable correlations should be computed on large samples such that the performance of one or two subjects will not unduly affect the result. No psychologist would trust a correlation based upon only seven subjects. Even when correlations are based upon 50 subjects, and this is a minimum figure, a few subjects who do well or badly on both tests can even then affect the result. Correlations become pretty reliable with a sample size of 100 or more.

2 The statistical significance of a correlation is important in determining its usefulness. Suppose we were to set out two columns with 100 randomly selected numbers in each column, selected either from tables of random numbers or by a random number generator in a computer. Then suppose that we compute the

correlation between them. Almost always it would be zero, i.e. there would be no relationship between the scores. Occasionally, however, by chance, a substantial correlation might occur.

When in the social sciences we correlate the scores on two tests, say, intelligence and mathematics, together and obtain a correlation of 0.31, how do we know that this is a meaningful correlation and not the result of chance and that the two variables are actually not positively correlated?

This question can be more precisely phrased by statisticians: if the true correlation between the variables is zero what is the probability of a correlation of size x arising?

From our examples it is clear that much depends upon sample size. With a small sample, where a few pairs of extreme scores in agreement strongly affect the size of the correlation, the correlation would have to be very large if it were to be regarded as unlikely to have arisen by chance. On the other hand with a sample size of 5,000 a small correlation, e.g. 0.09, would be most unlikely to be due to chance.

Fortunately, the probability of correlations of different sizes arising by chance (when the true correlation is zero) have been worked out for different sample sizes and it is possible to look this up in tables at the back of statistical texts.

So far I have explained the rationale of considering the probability of any correlation as having arisen simply by chance. The precise language of this must now be set out but the underlying statistical arguments will be not be necessary for the *Easy Guide*.

Significance

A correlation is said to be significant if it is greater than is likely to have arisen by chance.

Levels of significance

Two levels of significance are generally used: the 0.05 or 5 per cent level and the 0.01 or 1 per cent level.

Meaning of the 0.05 level significance   Suppose I have obtained a correlation of 0.32 between extraversion and swimming performance. I look this up under the appropriate sample size in the tables at the back of some statistical text. Suppose that in the 0.05 column I find the value 0.30. This means that there are less than five chances in a 100 that a correlation of 0.30 or bigger would have occurred, given the sample size. Thus my correlation is significant at the 0.05 level ($p < 0.05$). It is so unlikely to have arisen by chance that there is no point in considering the possibility.

Meaning of the 0.01 level of significance   I can look up my obtained correlation of 0.32 under the 0.01 level of significance. Suppose that there I find 0.35. This means that a correlation of 0.35 or larger could have arisen by chance only once in a hundred occasions. Since 0.32 is smaller, it means that it is significant at the 0.05 but not at the 0.01 level. Thus we cannot be completely confident about the correlation. The inequality $p < 0.01$ is used to indicate that a correlation is significant at the 0.01 level.

There are various points which should be made about significance levels and the interpretation of correlations.

1 To call a correlation significant because it is of a size such that there is a 5 per cent or less chance of its occurrence in random data is obviously arbitrary. Ten per cent or 3 per cent might have been chosen, for example. Nevertheless the 5 per cent level avoids reasonably well the error of giving meaningful interpretation to a statistical error.

2 The more significant a correlation is, the more confident one can be that there truly is a relationship between the variables. By highly significant we mean values well beyond the criterion value in the statistical tables.

3 As is obvious from our computational examples, we can have much more confidence in correlations obtained from large samples ($N > 100$).

4 Nevertheless replication of correlations on different samples is necessary to be certain that the results are not due to chance.

5 In large matrices of correlations by definition a few apparently significant correlations will have arisen by chance. Thus among 100 correlations one should by chance appear significant at the 0.01 level and 5 at the 0.05 level, since this is the meaning of significance. In matrices of several thousands of correlations there is no way of knowing which these are, although they are usually, in large samples, very small. That is why replication is important, as the chance correlations do not replicate.

6 Statistical significance which we have been discussing in this chapter must be distinguished from psychological significance. If a correlation is significant it means simply that it is unlikely to be due to chance. Suppose that in a sample of 5,000 children we had correlated a measure of reading ability and the extraversion level of the reading teachers and that a significant correlation of 0.089 had been obtained. Such a tiny correlation means that less than 1 per cent of the reading variance can be explained by teachers' extraversion. Thus the psychological significance or interpretation of this correlation is that there is virtually no relationship between these two variables.

Correlations can be illustrated in a scatter diagram and I shall conclude this chapter on correlations by setting out a scatter diagram and discussing its meaning and implications.

Scatter diagrams

In a scatter diagram of a correlation the scores of each subject are plotted on two axes, each representing one test. A computational example is given in Figure 2.1. As is obvious from the figure each person's location on the scattergram is given by the score on each of the two tests, X_1 on the vertical axis and X_2 on the horizontal. Our sample of data was chosen to illustrate the computing of correlations rather than to illustrate scattergrams. However, the data demonstrate one point clearly. The more nearly the points are to the diagonal (the 45° line) or are clustered close to it the higher the correlation. If a set of subjects had identical scores on two tests the scattergram would be a perfect straight line, just as the correlation would be +1. Figure 2.2 illustrates such a situation. This line is known as the regression line and when it is straight, as in the case of a perfect correlation, it enables us to predict the score on X_1 from scores on X_2 and vice versa. Normally when the correlation is not 1 the scores are clustered round this line, the tighter the cluster the higher the correlation. Then the regression has to be the best fit possible and predicting scores becomes riddled with error, the more so as the correlation departs from zero.

Regression is an important concept and will be further discussed later in the *Easy Guide*. Here I want to clarify the notion.

If we want to predict X_1 from X_2 then, as described above, a

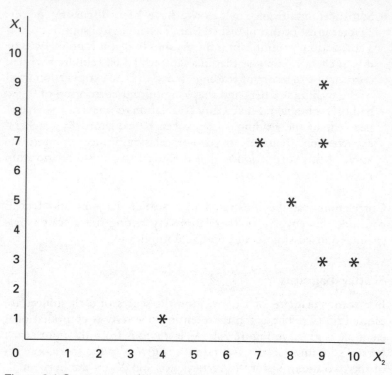

Figure 2.1 Scattergram of a correlation

regression line can be drawn, giving the best prediction, from a scattergram. This line can be described by a regression equation which in general form is given as

$$X_1(\text{predicted}) = a + bX_2 \qquad (2.8)$$

where X_1 is the score to be predicted on variable X_1; a is the intercept constant (to correct for differences in the means of the groups), called the intercept because it indicates the point on the axis cut by the regression line; b is the slope or regression constant which indicates the rate of change in X_1 as a function of the changes in X_2; and X_2 is the score on variable X_2. Clearly a and b need further explanation; they are calculated as shown by the following two equations.

$$b = r\left(\frac{\text{SD}_1}{\text{SD}_2}\right) \qquad (2.9)$$

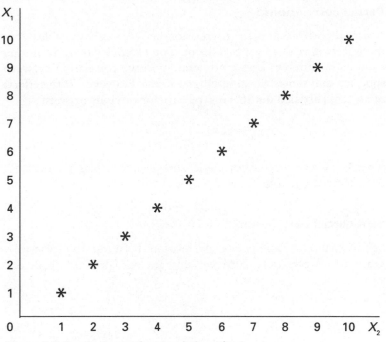

Figure 2.2 Scattergram of a correlation of +1

where r is the correlation between X_1 and X_2 and SD_1 and SD_2 are the standard deviations of the two sets of scores. Standard deviations, it will be remembered, are measures of the spread or variance in the scores (see formula (2.2)).

$$a = \text{mean}_1 - b(\text{mean}_2) \qquad (2.10)$$

where the means are the average of the groups. These equations indicate that given the means, standard deviations and correlation between two variables it is possible to predict one from the other. These statistics have all been fully dealt with in this chapter. It should also be noted that b, the slope, is identical to r, the correlation, when the scores on the two variables are expressed as standard scores (see formula (2.3)). When standard scores are thus used, a, the intercept, equals zero.

Correlations, variance, covariance and regression have all been carefully explained because they are essential to an understanding of factor analysis. To conclude, a brief account of partial and multiple correlations will also be valuable.

Partial correlations

A partial correlation is the correlation between two variables with the effects of a third cancelled out. For example, there is among children of different ages a moderate positive correlation between shoe size and scores on an intelligence test. However, if the effects of age are partialed out this disappears, for obvious reasons.

$$r_{12.3} = \frac{r_{12} - r_{13}r_{23}}{(1 - r_{13}^2)^{1/2}(1 - r_{23}^2)^{1/2}} \qquad (2.11)$$

where $r_{12.3}$ is the partial correlation between variables 1 and 2 with the effects of variable 3 partialed out.

Semipartial correlations

Semipartial correlations are correlation between two variables when the effects of a third variable are partialed out from one variable only.

$$r_{1(2.3)} = \frac{r_{12} - r_{13}r_{23}}{(1 - r_{23}^2)^{1/2}} \qquad (2.12)$$

where $r_{1(2.3)}$ is the correlation between variables 1 and 2 when the effects of variable 3 are partialed from variable 1 but not from variable 2.

Multiple correlations or regressions

It is possible to calculate the correlation between two or more variables and a criterion. This is known as a multiple correlation or regression. In multiple regression not only is the overall correlation between the set of variables and the criterion computed but so also are the β weights. β weights are the weightings for each variable to maximize the multiple correlation. It should be noted that these β weights – because they are designed to maximize the correlation in the sample – vary considerably from sample to sample and all multiple correlations should be replicated on new samples. If a huge sample has been obtained it is usual to split it and compute the multiple correlation in both groups.

$$R_{y.123}^2 = r_{y1}^2 + r_{y(2.1)}^2 + r_{y(3.12)}^2 \qquad (2.13)$$

where R is the multiple correlation; r_{y1} is the correlation between variables y and 1; $r_{y(2.1)}$ is the semipartial correlation between y and 2 with 1 partialed from 2; and $r_{y(3.12)}$ is the semipartial correlation between y and 3 with 1 and 2 partialed from 3.

In this chapter I have set out and exemplified the algebra of some statistical terms which it is most helpful to understand in the study of factor analysis, many of them being fundamental to it. Most important of all is the need to grasp the nature of correlations and test variance.

Chapter 3

Principal components analysis

We are now in a position to understand factor analysis: all the necessary statistical concepts have been explained in Chapter 2. In this chapter I shall work through an example of principal components analysis. However, before I do I want to make a few more general points about factor analysis.

AIM OF FACTOR ANALYSIS

As was discussed in the first chapter of the *Easy Guide* the aim of most factor analyses is to simplify a matrix of correlations such that they can be explained in terms of a few underlying factors. When Spearman (1904) introduced the technique the simplest computational methods had to be used. However, over the years, as calculating machines and computers became more powerful, a number of different computational methods have been developed and there are now several different kinds of factor analysis which will be discussed in Chapter 4.

In this chapter I shall explicate principal components analysis. This type of analysis has been chosen for several reasons. First, as shall be seen both in this chapter and the next where some of its characteristics are discussed, the algebra and computation of principal components is not difficult. Furthermore, the computational methods used in this chapter make absolutely clear the basis of the assertions that factors account for variance and explain correlations. Thus, once the computation of principal components has been understood, the nature of factor analysis becomes self-evident.

This, indeed, is the reason for so carefully going through principal components analysis in the *Easy Guide*. In practice researchers use computer packages to carry out factor analyses and in these matrix algebra rather than the method explained in this chapter is used. However, factor analysis without understanding is an unmitigated evil in the social sciences and these packages guarantee no insight. Indeed, as Cattell (1978) has argued, many published factor analyses are technically inadequate and their results misleading.

PRINCIPAL COMPONENTS ANALYSIS

My description of principal components analysis will be the essential minimum necessary for understanding. The best description can be found in Nunnally (1978), although as is pointed out later in this chapter certain aspects of his description are misleading. I also describe this method in some detail in my *Handbook of Psychological Testing* (Kline 1992). First some special terms need to be defined.

The characteristic equation

The aim of principal components analysis is to be able to estimate the correlation matrix and this can be done by finding the characteristic equation of the matrix. This requires two sets of values:

1 the characteristic vectors of the matrix, also called latent vectors or eigenvectors – a vector is simply a column or row of numbers in a matrix. The symbol for a characteristic vector is V_a;
2 characteristic roots, also called latent roots or eigenvalues – the symbol for a characteristic root is l_a.

Definition of a characteristic vector

A characteristic vector is a column of weights each applicable to one of the variables in the matrix. Thus if there were six variables there would be six weights in the first vector – V_a, V_b and so on. The corresponding factor loadings, F_a, F_b, can be obtained by multiplying each element of the vector by the square root of the corresponding eigenvalue.

Definition of characteristic root or eigenvalue

The sum of squares of the factor loadings of each factor reflects the proportion of variance explained by each factor. This total amount of variance is the characteristic root or eigenvalue l_a for the factor.

The larger the eigenvalue the more variance is explained by the factor.

Computing principal components

Thus to compute principal components eigenvalues and eigenvectors or characteristic roots and values must be computed. The original method of Hotelling (1933) will be explicated because of its clarity and simplicity, although the normalization procedures are not exactly the same.

Principle of the method

The eigenvectors and roots are derived by an iterative solution. A vector is tried out and tested against a criterion set of values. To the extent that it diverges from the criterion, the first trial vector is modified to produce a second vector and so on until the solution converges, i.e. until additional iterations produce virtually identical results.

Iteration

In the iterative approach characteristic vectors are obtained one at a time. Once the iterative solution has converged, the eigenvalue can be calculated from the vector and the same iterative method is then used to search for successive vectors.

This is the basis of principal components analysis. How this is actually done will be described in a series of steps on a simple correlation matrix which is given in Table 3.1.

Table 3.1 Correlation matrix

	IQ	Verbal	Maths	Space
IQ	1.0	0.4	0.3	0.2
Verbal	0.4	1.0	0.2	0.1
Maths	0.3	0.2	1.0	0.3
Space	0.2	0.1	0.3	1.0
Total	1.9	1.7	1.8	1.6

Step 1: Sum the coefficients in each column These four sums are a vector U_{a1}. Thus $U_{a1} = (1.9, 1.7, 1.8, 1.6)$.

Step 2: Normalize U_{a1} This is done by squaring and adding the column sums in U_{a1} and then dividing each element by the square root of the sum of squares. The first trial characteristic vector, V_{a1}, is this normalized U_{a1}. Thus we compute $3.61 + 2.89 + 3.24 + 2.56 = 12.3$. The square root of 12.3 is 3.51 and so we then divide the elements in U_{a1} by 3.51 to normalize it and produce the first trial vector V_{a1}. Thus V_{a1} is $(0.54, 0.48, 0.51, 0.46)$.

Step 3: Produce the second trial vector V_{a2} The elements of V_{a1} are accumulatively multiplied by the first row of R, the correlation matrix, to obtain the first element in a new vector, U_{a2}. The successive multiplication is carried out as follows.

First element
$0.54 \times 1 + 0.48 \times 0.4 + 0.51 \times 0.3 + 0.46 \times 0.2 = 0.97$
Second element
$0.54 \times 0.4 + 0.48 \times 1 + 0.51 \times 0.2 + 0.46 \times 0.1 = 0.85$
Third element
$0.54 \times 0.3 + 0.48 \times 0.2 + 0.51 \times 1 + 0.46 \times 0.3 = 0.90$
Fourth element
$0.54 \times 0.2 + 0.48 \times 0.1 + 0.51 \times 0.3 + 0.46 \times 1 = 0.77$

Step 4: Normalize U_{a2} Square and add the elements of U_{a2}. Divide each element by the square root of the sum of the squared elements. This produces the second trial characteristic vector V_{a2}. Thus we compute: $0.94 + 0.72 + 0.81 + 0.59 = 3.06$. The square root of 3.06 is 1.75 and thus the elements in U_{a2} are divided by 1.75 to produce the second trial characteristic vector $V_{a2} = (0.55, 0.49, 0.51, 0.44)$.

Step 5: Compare the first two trial vectors Although they are highly similar they are not the same and it is necessary to produce a third trial vector.

Step 6: Produce the third trial vector The third trial vector is produced as was the second.

First element
$0.55 \times 1 + 0.49 \times 0.4 + 0.51 \times 0.3 + 0.44 \times 0.2 = 0.98$

Second element
  $0.55 \times 0.4 + 0.49 \times 1 + 0.51 \times 0.2 + 0.44 \times 0.1 = 0.85$
Third element
  $0.55 \times 0.3 + 0.49 \times 0.2 + 0.51 \times 1 + 0.44 \times 0.3 = 0.90$
Fourth element
  $0.55 \times 0.2 + 0.49 \times 0.1 + 0.51 \times 0.3 + 0.44 \times 1 = 0.75$

The last column is the vector U_{a3}.

Step 7: Normalize U_{a3}   This is done exactly as was the case with U_{a2}. Thus we compute: $0.96 + 0.72 + 0.81 + 0.56 = 3.05$. The square root of 3.05 is 1.75 and thus the elements in U_{a3} are divided by 1.75 to produce the third trial characteristic vector $V_{a3} = (0.56, 0.49, 0.51, 0.43)$.

Step 8: Compare the second and third trial vectors   Within the limits of accuracy of two decimal places, correcting upwards if the third decimal is greater than 0.5, it is reasonable to argue that the solutions have converged. Of course, a greater accuracy of convergence would be expected when using high speed computers to compute real data with many variables. In fact the criterion for convergence is that the sum of the squared differences between the pairs of elements in the two vectors is less than 0.00001. However, for purposes of explanation this convergence is satisfactory.

Step 9: V_{a2} and V_{a3} are regarded as identical (convergence having been reached) V_{a2} becomes the first characteristic vector of the matrix. The square root of the sum of squares in U_{a3} equals the first characteristic root or eigenvalue, l_a. The factor loadings are obtained by multiplying the elements in the first characteristic vector by the square root of the eigenvalue l_a. Thus the first principal component has been extracted (Table 3.2). There is clearly a large general factor accounting for the correlations in this matrix.

Step 10: Obtain the second principal component   The second factor is obtained in the same way as the first. Thus the characteristic vector, the characteristic root and the factor loadings are computed as above, trial characteristic vectors being extracted until convergence occurs. However, these vectors and roots are extracted not from the original correlation matrix but from a

Table 3.2 The first principal component

Variable	Factor 1
IQ	0.74
Verbal	0.65
Maths	0.67
Space	0.57
Eigenvalue	1.76[a]

Note: [a] The sum of squares of the factor loadings, which equals within the limits of accuracy the eigenvalue calculated from the trial vector.

residual matrix after the first factor has been partialed out. This demonstrates what it means to say that a factor accounts for variance in a correlation matrix.

Step 11: Obtain the residual matrix (R_1) The residual coefficient corresponding to the original correlation is obtained in the following way. The loadings for the two variables on the first component are multiplied. This is done for all possible pairs of variables and produces a matrix of cross products. In each diagonal space is the square of the factor loading. This matrix of cross products is then subtracted element by element from the original correlation matrix and the result is the residual matrix with the first component partialed out. These processes will now be illustrated on our sample matrix. I shall compute the cross products and diagonals in the same order as on the original matrix:

IQ/V	$0.74 \times 0.65 = 0.48$		IQ/M	$0.74 \times 0.67 = 0.50$
V/IQ	$= 0.48$		V/M	$0.65 \times 0.67 = 0.44$
M/IQ	$0.74 \times 0.67 = 0.50$		M/V	$= 0.44$
S/IQ	$0.74 \times 0.57 = 0.42$		S/V	$0.65 \times 0.57 = 0.37$

IQ/S	$0.74 \times 0.57 = 0.42$	Diag $= 0.55$
V/S	$0.65 \times 0.57 = 0.37$	Diag $= 0.43$
M/S	$0.67 \times 0.57 = 0.38$	Diag $= 0.45$
S/M	$= 0.38$	Diag $= 0.32$

Step 12: Subtract the new elements from the original correlations Thus we obtain the residual matrix given in Table 3.3. The meaning of reflection and the nature of the residual matrix are now discussed.

Each diagonal element is the variance remaining after the first

Table 3.3 The residual matrix

	IQ	Verbal	Maths[a]	Space[a]
IQ	0.46	−0.08	−0.20	−0.22
Verbal	−0.08	0.57	−0.24	−0.27
Maths[a]	−0.20	−0.24	0.55	−0.08
Space[a]	−0.22	−0.27	−0.08	0.68

Note: [a] Indicates that the factors will be reflected.

component is partialed out. Thus if we examine the residual matrix we can see that the first component has accounted for 55 per cent of the variance in the IQ test, 43 per cent of the variance in the verbal test, 45 per cent of the variance in the maths test and 32 per cent of the variance in the space measure. This indicates clearly what it means to say that a factor accounts for variance. This first factor incidentally must be a general ability or intelligence factor. It accounts for much of the variance in all the tests other than the spatial test. With so much variance accounted for, other components would be necessarily small.

The other elements are partial covariances between the variables, covariances with the effect of the first factor partialed out. As each factor is partialed out the coefficients in the residual matrix become smaller and smaller until all variance in the matrix is extracted. In the case of a four variable matrix this would occur with four components.

The residual matrix has to be reflected because, with the effects of the first factor partialed out the sum of elements in each column differs from zero only by rounding error. However, if the spatial and maths rows and columns are reflected, i.e. all signs changed other than the diagonals, this overcomes the difficulty and maximizes the size of the vector. This is no statistical trick since when the loadings have been computed for the second component the loadings of the reflected variables are given negative signs. The reflected residual matrix becomes as shown in Table 3.4.

Table 3.4 The reflected residual matrix

	0.46	−0.08	0.20	0.22
	−0.08	0.57	0.24	0.27
	0.20	0.24	0.55	−0.08
	0.22	0.27	−0.08	0.68
Total	0.80	1.00	0.91	1.09

Step 13: Produce U_{b1} The second component is then extracted from the residual matrix exactly as the first component was obtained from the correlation matrix. The column sums of the reflected residual matrix are the first trial characteristic vector U_{b1}.

Step 14: Normalize U_{b1} This is done by squaring and adding the column sums in U_{b1} and dividing each element by the square root of the sum of squares. Thus we compute: $0.64 + 1.0 + 0.83 + 1.19 = 3.66$. The square root of 3.66 is 1.91 and therefore dividing the elements of U_{b1} by 1.91 we obtain the first trial vector $V_{b1} = (0.42, 0.52, 0.48, 0.57)$.

From then on the procedure is exactly as before until the second trial vectors converge. Because the spatial variable was reflected all the signs of the principal component loadings in that column and row will be changed. However, as will be discussed this makes no difference to the meaning of the factors.

I have illustrated the computations of principal components on a very simple matrix and the actual results are inevitably somewhat unrealistic. Nevertheless the computations are sufficient to illustrate clearly the nature of principal components which I shall discuss below.

Number of components to extract

As was mentioned in our discussion of the residual matrix, one can go on extracting components until the coefficients in the residual matrix are so small that it is clear that there is little variance or covariance to account for. If the full number of components are extracted (as many components as there are variables in the matrix) then all the variance is extracted and the residual matrix will contain zeros. Of course the *last* few components will be very small, i.e. will have small loadings.

SOME GENERAL POINTS ABOUT FACTOR ANALYSIS

With the computation of principal components in mind I shall now make some more general points about factor analysis and define factors with a little more precision than was done in our introductory chapter.

A distinction between components and factors

These terms are often used as if they were interchangeable and in the *Easy Guide* I sometimes refer to components as factors. In fact there is a real distinction which should be understood, although with large data sets in practice it becomes trivial as Harman (1976) has shown.

Components are real factors because they are derived directly from the correlation matrix. Common factors of factor analysis are hypothetical because they are estimated from the data. These methods will be discussed in Chapter 4. In fact the principal axes method of factor analysis is identical to that of principal components except that instead of unity in the diagonals some other estimate of communality is inserted. This means that while the principal components method explains all the variance in a matrix the principal axes method does not. This, theoretically, is an advantage, because it is unlikely that factors could explain all the variance in any given matrix and, since all correlations contain error, the full account of principal components must be contaminated by error. However, as mentioned above, Harman (1976) has shown that with large matrices the principal components and principal axes methods are virtually identical.

Definition of a factor   A linear combination of variables, any combination, constitutes a factor.

What is required in factor analysis is an combination of variables so weighted as to account for the variance in the correlations. Factor analytic methods, of which principal components is one example, are designed for this purpose.

Definition of factor loadings   As was mentioned in Chapter 1, factor loadings are the correlations of the variables with the factor, the weighted combination of variables which best explains the variance.

In a large matrix it is highly unlikely that all the variance could be explained by one factor. Thus, as was seen in our example, after the extraction of the first factor a second factor can be extracted and so on until the residual matrix becomes negligible.

As was clear from the worked example, in extracting the second factor, the first factor was partialled out of the matrix. The residual matrix consisted of partial variances and covariances. This means that the second factor must be uncorrelated with the first factor. The same applies to any subsequent factors. Thus iterative factoring must yield a set of uncorrelated factors.

It has already been pointed out that with principal component analysis it is possible to take out as many components as variables, thus exhausting all the variance in the matrix. However, since one of the aims of exploratory factor analysis is to explain a matrix of correlations with as few factors as is possible, it is usual to take out less than this number. How many factors should be extracted is a complex matter and this will be discussed in later chapters of this book, especially Chapters 4 and 5.

There are certain other characteristics of factors and components which should be mentioned at this juncture.

1 As has been pointed out, the factor loadings are the correlations of the variables with the factors. The squared factor loading of variables indicates the percentage of variance of that variable explained by the factor. Thus to take our worked example, the first principal component explains 55 per cent of the variance in the IQ test and 42 per cent of the variance in the verbal test.

2 The average of the squared loadings of a factor shows the percentage of variance in the correlation matrix explained by that factor. Thus to take our example: the sum of squares is 1.74; this is the eigenvalue or the characteristic root. Now, 1.74/4 = 0.43 and thus the first principal component explains 43 per cent of the variance in the correlation matrix.

3 The sum of the average squared loadings on all factors indicates the proportion of variance in the matrix explained by the factors. In the case of principal components, when all factors are extracted all the variance is explained. When, as is usual, only some of the factors are extracted the more variance which the factors explain the better.

4 The loadings in the rows of a factor matrix can be squared and summed. The sum of squares for each row indicates the proportion of variance in each variable which the factors can explain. This is known as h^2, the communality. The higher the communality the more the particular set of factors explain the variance of the variable.

5 β weights are the weights to be applied to a set of variables if we want to maximize the correlation between the set and some

criterion. The correlation between several variables and a criterion is known as the multiple correlation.

When factors are uncorrelated as in the case of principal components analysis, factor loadings are not only the correlation of the variable with the factor, as has been previously discussed, they are also the β weights for predicting the variable from the factor.

So far I have discussed the general characteristics of factors which clearly apply to principal components as well as to factors produced by other methods some of which will be discussed in the next chapter. However, there are certain mathematical characteristics which are peculiar to principal components and which make the technique so valuable in the analysis of data in psychology and the social sciences.

1 As is clear from the worked example, principal components emerge ordered by the proportion of variance for which they account. No other method of extracting factors could yield factors, at any stage of extraction, which explained more variance than components.

   In brief, principal components maximize the variance explained for any number of factors.
2 The variance explained by any component (the sum of the squared loadings, see (2) in the previous list) equals the eigenvalue of the component. This divided by the number of variables indicates the proportion of variance explained by the component.
3 Eigenvalues must be zero or positive. If they are not there must be error or inconsistency in the correlation matrix.
4 The number of positive eigenvalues represents the number of components necessary to explain the variance in the correlation matrix. However, in principal components analysis, as has been shown, there are as many components as variables. However, the last few components are very small and contribute little to the variance. How many factors to extract will be discussed in the next chapter.
5 The sum of eigenvalues equals the sum of the diagonal elements in the matrix. Thus in principal components analysis the sum equals the number of variables. This allows the calculation of the proportion of variance accounted for by a factor or a group of factors (see (2) in the previous list).

6 Principal components are uncorrelated (orthogonal) linear combinations of actual scores.

7 In most cases the first principal component explains far more variance than the other components.

8 If most of the correlations in the correlation matrix are positive, the first principal component has large positive loadings on most of the variables. This is called a general factor.

That the first principal component is usually a general factor is an artifact of the method, as is evident from our example. It is thus inadmissible, but it is often done, to use the first principal component as evidence for the presence of a general factor.

9 Subsequent factors are usually bipolar, that is they have both negative and positive loadings. Again, as was evident from the first residual matrix and the necessity for reflection in our example, this is an artifact of the method and this bipolarity should not be interpreted as reflecting anything in the original data.

10 As is made clear in (8) and (9), the fact that principal components analysis produces as a result of its computational algebra an arbitrary general factor followed by bipolar factors makes interpretation of results difficult. This does not apply only to the general factor. Factors with many positive and negative loadings are also hard to interpret. For this reason methods of simplifying principal components analyses have been developed. This is done by rotation of factors. However, this is such an important topic that it will be dealt with separately in Chapter 5.

REPRODUCING THE CORRELATIONS AMONG THE VARIABLES FROM THE FACTOR LOADINGS

One of the tests of the quality of a factor analysis is to see how accurately the correlations can be reproduced from the factors. Indeed it is this ability to reproduce the correlations which further demonstrates that factors account for variance. Even more importantly it is this ability which makes factors useful in research. Thus it enables us to deal with a few variables, the factors, rather than all the original variables. Factor analysis yields a true simplification of the data, provided that the correlations can be reproduced.

If all the principal components of a matrix are extracted, then the correlations between the variables can be perfectly reproduced.

However, this is not a simplification since there are as many components as variables. In practice, of course, only a few components are extracted, the largest in terms of variance accounted for, and these should be able to account for the correlations partially. A good test of the adequacy of an analysis is to reproduce the correlations and then subtract them from their originals. What is left is a residual matrix. If the elements in this are small – little above zero – then the analysis is satisfactory.

The following equation shows how correlations are reproduced from factor loadings, where two factors have been extracted.

$$r_{xy} = r_{x1y1} + r_{x2y2} \qquad (3.1)$$

where r_{xy} is the correlation of variables x and y; r_{x1y1} is the cross product of the factor loadings of variables x and y on factor 1; and r_{x2y2} is the cross product of the factor loadings of variables x and y on factor 2. Obviously if more factors were extracted the cross products from the other factor loadings would be included in the equation.

SUMMARY OF THE MAIN POINTS OF PRINCIPAL COMPONENTS ANALYSIS

1 Principal components analysis is one method of condensing a matrix of correlations.
2 Principal components explain all the variance in any particular correlation matrix, including the error variance (see Chapter 4).
3 Principal components should strictly be distinguished from factors which are hypothetical, but see Chapter 4.
4 There are as many components as variables but only the largest are extracted, but see Chapter 4.
5 The first principal component accounts for the most variance and the components are ordered in size as they are extracted.
6 The eigenvalues of each component indicate how much variance it accounts for.
7 The eigenvalue of any component divided by the number of variables indicates the proportion of variance it accounts for.
8 All eigenvalues must be zero or positive. If they are not there is error or the matrix should not be factored.
9 The factor loadings are the correlations of the variables with the factors.

10 The factor loadings are also the beta weights for predicting the variables from the factors. This is because principal components are uncorrelated or orthogonal.

11 The sum of squares of the rows of a factor matrix indicates how much variance in each variable the factors can account for.

12 The factor loading squared indicates how much variance a factor can account for in that variable.

13 The original correlations can be reproduced by cross-multiplication of the factor loadings.

14 The more accurate the reproduction (the smaller the residual matrix) the better the analysis.

15 Principal components analysis generally produces one general factor followed by bipolar factors.

16 Because the factors mentioned in (15) are algebraic artefacts they must usually be simplified before they can be interpreted (see Chapter 5).

Chapter 4

Other methods of factor analysis

In this chapter I shall discuss and describe other methods of factor analysis and compare them with the principal components method. Before I begin this comparison it will be helpful to discuss what was left implicit, although perfectly obvious, in the last chapter, i.e. the factor analytic model of variance.

THE FACTOR ANALYTIC MODEL OF VARIANCE

In the factor analytic account of variance there are three uncorrelated components.

1 *Common variance*. This is the proportion of the variance which can be explained by common factors.
2 *Specific variance*. This is the variance which is particular to a test or variable. In the case of a test, for example, specific variance can arise from the particular form of the items in the test, especially if they are different from those in other tests, and from the particular content.
3 *Error variance*. Almost all measurement, not only in psychology, is subject to random error. With psychological tests the reliability, the correlation of the test with itself or its internal consistency, is an index of measurement error. Squaring this correlation and subtracting from 100 gives the amount of error variance. Thus if a test has a reliability of 0.9, there is 19 per cent error variance in the scores.

Unique variance

In principal components analysis error and specific variance are not separated out. They are known as the unique variance and are given by

$$U \text{ (unique variance)} = h^2 - 1 \qquad (4.1)$$

where h^2 is the communality.

It will be remembered from Chapter 3 that the communality of a variable was calculated by squaring and adding the elements in the relevant row of the factor matrix. Where all the principal components have been extracted, including the very small ones, the communality is, of course, unity.

One approach to separating error from specific variance is not to insert 1 in the diagonal as is done for principal components but to insert the reliability of the test. As was shown above the reliabilities exclude error variance, thus any variance not explained by common factors should be specific. This problem of specific and error variance will be discussed later in this chapter when the different methods of factor analysis are examined.

Other methods of condensation

In the last chapter I described principal components analysis. However, this is, as I hope is now clear, only one method of condensation. Although it maximizes the variance accounted for in the correlation matrix, it has an important source of difficulty. The problem is that it accounts for all the variance in the matrix to which it is applied. Since any given matrix must contain some error, however small, this is a disadvantage. Furthermore since, as was discussed in the opening chapter, the aim of factor analysis is to discover important underlying structures this ability to explain all the variance is not promising.

To some extent this can be countered by not extracting all the components. Nevertheless this does not entirely avoid the problem of the error variance, because of the fact that 1s are placed in the diagonal.

For these reasons especially, other methods of condensation, i.e. reducing the rank of the matrix, have been developed and these must now be discussed.

Common factor analysis

Cattell (1978) prefers to work with common factors rather than components even though in large matrices differences between the two solutions are trivial (Harman 1976).

Distinction between components and factors

Although this was briefly mentioned in Chapter 3, it will be convenient to clarify this distinction here. There are several important differences.

1 *Components are real factors.* In the principal components method the factors are actual combinations of variables. The factor loadings are the correlations of these combinations with the factors.

2 *Common factors are hypothetical.* Common factors have to be estimated from actual variables and to obtain them mathematical procedures must be used which specify factors in terms of common variance.

3 *Communalities must be less than unity.* Because factors are concerned with common variance, it follows that the communalities, the diagonal elements of the correlation matrix, must be less than one.

4 *Common and unique variance are separated.* At the beginning of this chapter common and unique variance were distinguished. When 1s are placed in the diagonals, as is the case with principal components analysis, this separation is not complete. This is because the variables themselves determine the factors but the variables are composed of unique and common variance. In common factor analysis unique and common variance are separated.

5 *Advantages of common factor analysis.* From these comparisons a number of advantages of common factor analysis compared with principal components analysis become evident.

   (a) It is clearly useful to separate out common and unique variance since unique variance is of no scientific interest.

   (b) That factors are hypothetical rather than real is an advantage. A factor may account for the correlations among variables without being completely defined by them. This makes them of some theoretical interest. For example if we argue that extraversion accounts for much of the variance in a matrix it is odd if it is completely defined by the variables in a matrix, as is the case with principal components analysis.

Principal factor analysis

There are various different methods of common factor analysis, which is a generic term, but I shall discuss only the most widely used in the *Easy Guide*. I shall begin with principal factor analysis.

Principal factor analysis is identical to principal components analysis except that instead of 1s in the diagonal of the correlation matrix the communalities are estimated. How this is carried out will be discussed below. Although it may seem a trivial problem, in fact there is considerable dispute how this should be done and its importance is attested by the fact that the choice of communalities affects the number of factors which are extracted, since, unlike principal components analysis, fewer factors than variables are extracted.

Iterative computation of communalities

In this approach developed by Thurstone the reliabilities of the variables are placed in the diagonals and the matrix is submitted to principal factor analysis until the residual matrix is minute. The number of factors to reach this point is regarded as the correct number of factors to explain the variance.

The communality h^2 is then computed for all variables (the sums of squares of the rows of the factor loadings). These communalities are compared with the original estimates in the diagonals. Unless the differences are tiny these h^2 values are put into the diagonals and principal factors are again computed, the same number of factors being extracted. This cycle is repeated again and again until the h^2 values no longer differ from the diagonals. The factor loadings which were used in the final iteration are regarded as correct.

Although this iterative method is used in a number of factor analytic methods, Nunnally (1978) points out several difficulties with it which should be mentioned.

1 It is assumed that the number of factors emerging from the first iteration is correct, for this number is extracted in all further iterations. There is no proof that this is indeed the case.
2 Furthermore the first estimate that was put in the diagonals of the

correlation matrix actually affects the final solution, again casting doubt on the method. Indeed it must be realized that there is an inextricable link between the number of factors extracted and the communalities (Cattell 1978).

3 Finally iterative methods can lead to communalities greater than unity which makes no sense.

All this means that factor analyses and factor loadings should not be regarded as eternal truths graven by computers. However, as will be shown in later chapters of this book, despite these problems, replicable and trustworthy results can be obtained. Nevertheless it is essential that all users of factor analysis and those who read and evaluate the findings are aware of these difficulties.

Estimating communalities using the squared multiple correlation

The squared multiple correlation (SMC) for estimating each variable from all the others in the matrix is obtained by computing the multiple correlations between each variable and the other variables in the matrix (the formula is given in Chapter 2). The squares of these are placed in the diagonals.

Nunnally (1978) has pointed out a number of difficulties with the SMC estimate of communalities of which the most important are the following.

1 In artificial matrices where the factors are known factor analyses in which the SMCs are placed in the diagonals fail to reproduce the factors. This is sufficient evidence to contra-indicate their use.

2 In large matrices SMCs tend to approach unity.

For these reasons Nunnally argues that SMCs may be a useful starting point for the iterative procedures of Thurstone's method.

Statistically significant factors

As was argued in our discussion of the iterative method an important problem concerned the number of factors to be extracted. In terms of matrix algebra, the extraction of factors which will account for the variance in the matrix and yet are fewer in number than the original variables is called reducing the rank of the matrix.

Thus a ten variable matrix may be reduced in rank to three if three factors can be shown to account for the variance. Indeed it is possible to see factor analysis as a method of reducing the rank of a matrix, which Thurstone (1947) indeed argued.

This matrix reduction was suggested by Thurstone as a basis for overcoming the problem of extracting the correct number of factors. He argued that after the first factor was extracted the significance of the residual matrix should be tested. This tests whether the residual coefficients were such as could arise by chance if they were really zero. If it was significant a second factor is extracted and so on until the residual matrix is no longer statistically significant. The number of factors extracted at this point is declared as the rank of the matrix and the factors are regarded as significant.

However, as Nunnally (1978) has argued, although these statistical tests are mathematically sound and elegant, they are not rigorous and do not in fact describe the matrix in the most economical terms. For practical factor analysis they are not therefore ideal.

In fact the extraction of the correct number of factors is a vital part of good factor analytic procedures and how this is done in modern factor analyses is discussed in the next chapter. Here Thurstone's method was mentioned because it forms part of his pioneering approach to the problems of factor analysis, as does his iterative methods of finding the communalities to be placed in the diagonals. Thus a combination of these two methods (if the statistical approach were not too lenient) would be powerful: fix the number of factors and iterate the communalities using this number. Indeed this is essentially the method proposed by Cattell (1978), although he fixes the number of factors by a procedure which will be discussed in the next chapter.

So far in this discussion I have examined some of the problems involved in the computing of principal factors. As can be seen these involve the estimation of the communalities and the extraction of the correct number of factors.

One approach to the solution of these problems and the one currently in favour is to use the maximum likelihood method of condensation and this will be described later in this chapter. Before I do this, however, it is worth noting two methods which attempt to overcome the problems of the diagonal entries in the correlation matrix by avoiding their use. These are not common methods but it is useful to be aware of them should they be used in any research papers.

Minimum residual factor analysis

Comrey (1962) and Harman (1976) have both developed factoring methods which make no use of the diagonal entries. These are known as minimum residual factor analyses. As Nunnally (1978) points out, these two methods are highly similar although Comrey extracts one factor at a time while Harman extracts a specified number of factors before the residual matrix is examined.

In principal components analysis, as has been seen, each factor is extracted to explain as much variance as possible. In minimum residual analysis factors are extracted against the criterion of minimizing the sum of squared off diagonal residuals after factors are extracted. The computer algorithms ignore the diagonal entries. Comrey's method, indeed, is a highly similar iterative procedure to that of principal components analysis, except that it avoids using the diagonal entries.

Harman's (1976) method, minimizing the residual matrix for a specified group of factors, is regarded as a more elegant method than that of Comrey and ought in principle, according to Nunnally (1978), to lead to a better fit than the single factor approach. However, there are a number of difficulties with the method, as Harman admits. The most severe of these concerns the number of factors. The method is efficient only if the correct number of factors is already known. In exploratory factor analyses this is rarely the case. Obviously, if the fit is not good (i.e. the residual matrix is not approaching zero) different numbers of factors can be extracted. But this is a tedious procedure, even with modern computing facilities.

In addition, communalities larger than one can arise (although a correcting factor can be used) and on occasions highly misleading solutions can be obtained.

As was mentioned earlier in this section, these minimum residual methods have not been much used despite the fact that they overcome the difficulty of estimating the communalities in the diagonals of the matrix. Nunnally argues that the reason for this is not the occasional problems with the methods of misleading solutions but rather the fact that they were highly complex and known only to statistical specialists rather than to practical users of factor analysis. Of course this is a problem with the whole of factor analysis and is one of the reasons for writing this *Easy Guide*.

Finally it is interesting to note that both Nunnally (1978) and

Cattell (1978) argue that minimum residual methods are useful for establishing communalities prior to a standard principal factor analysis.

Maximum likelihood factor analysis

This method of factor analysis has become popular in recent years partly because of the development of some powerful multivariate statistical computer packages of which this forms a part. Much of this work was carried out by Joreskog and his colleagues (Joreskog 1973) and will be further discussed when we come to scrutinize confirmatory factor analysis in Chapter 6.

Maximum likelihood factor analysis differs from principal components analysis and other methods of condensation in a number of ways which need to be described.

1 Maximum likelihood factor analysis obtains by successive factoring a set of factors each of which in turn explains as much variance as possible in the *population* correlation matrix, as estimated from the sample correlation matrix.

This, it must be noted, sharply separates it from principal components analysis which explains as much variance as possible in the observed or *sample* matrix. For this reason maximum likelihood analysis is regarded as a statistical method because, as is the case with all inferential statistics, inferences are made from sample to population. Clearly, therefore, large and adequate samples are essential.

2 Maximum likelihood analysis is particularly suited to confirmatory analysis which will be described in Chapter 6. However, it can be used simply as a method of condensation analogous to principal component or principal factor analysis.

3 Maximum likelihood factor analysis, as a method of condensation, is usually used to search for factors. However, when test reliabilities and thus communalities are high the difference between maximum likelihood factor analysis and principal components analysis is trivial, as indeed is the case with principal component and principal factor analysis.

In the test development, for example, of a five factor personality test the same items were selected by principal component analysis and by the maximum likelihood method. The only differences in the solutions were found in those items which had low loadings on the factors (Kline and Lapham 1991). This was not some isolated phenomenon. Nunnally (1978) points out that when communalities are high there are few differences between principal components analysis and maximum likelihood factor analysis.

4 The strongest argument for using maximum likelihood analysis lies in the fact that it has statistical tests for the significance of each factor as it is extracted. This is contrasted by the advocates of the method with the fact that other factoring methods are essentially convenient algorithms.

5 The mathematics of maximum likelihood methods are highly complex and will not be explicated in this *Easy Guide*. In fact, to quote Nunnally (1978), they need 'a solid grounding in calculus, higher algebra and matrix algebra'. They are explained with as much clarity as is possible in Mulaik (1972).

The fact that maximum likelihood factor analysis produces results so similar to the principal factors and components method, when used as a method of condensation, means that to use more simple methods is by no means ruled out. The one advantage it possess over other methods of condensation is the power of its statistical tests. This has made it obligatory, virtually, for statistically minded psychologists, although, as will be discussed in the next chapter, non-statistical methods for selecting the correct number of factors seem highly efficient.

Finally it should be noted that even with modern computers computing time and costs are greater with maximum likelihood methods than with the less complex methods already described. Where this is important the simpler methods are perfectly satisfactory, as will become clear in the next chapter.

It must be stressed that this discussion of maximum likelihood analysis is concerned with its use as a method of condensation in exploratory analysis. In fact its main use is in confirmatory analysis, in which hypotheses are put to the test. This will be discussed in Chapter 6.

Before leaving this chapter on methods of condensation, two other methods deserve to be discussed albeit briefly simply so that if readers come across research in which they were used they will know how to evaluate them.

Image analysis

In image analysis it is argued that the common core of the variables is what can be predicted by multiple regression of all the other variables on to each variable. Thus the multiple regression between variables 1 and all others is computed (see Chapter 2) followed by the multiple regression of variable 2 with all others and so on throughout the matrix, resulting in a set of predicted variables. This rationale, as has been mentioned, was used in the development of the SMC as being the best diagonal entry for factor analysis.

The image covariance matrix

From these predicted variable scores an image covariance (see Chapter 2) matrix, rather than an image correlation matrix, is computed. This covariance matrix is then subjected to factor analysis by any of the methods of condensation which have been described.

The image factor loadings

The question now arises what the factor loadings in image analysis are. Clearly they are not correlations with the variables. The image analysis factor loadings are covariances of the image variables with a linear combination of the image variables. This is not easy to understand and makes interpretation tricky, although Nunnally suggests that they may be interpreted as if they were ordinary factor loadings.

Problems with image analysis

I shall not discuss image analysis in any further detail because there are some problems with it which overcome its purported advantage – namely that it provides a unique solution to accounting for the common variance among variables (because the image scores are only what can be predicted), thus eliminating error.

A major difficulty is that in artificial matrices where the factors are known image analysis is not always able to reproduce the factors. Furthermore the notion of the common core in image analysis is restricted, as is the case with principal components analysis, to the particular set of variables. Furthermore, as Cattell

(1978) has argued, the specific variance in each test is included in the image variables and this reduces the value of the procedure. Finally despite the brilliance of the notion of image analysis in general the results are little different from those of more direct factoring methods.

α factor analysis

The aim of α factor analysis is to yield factor scores (scores based on the factors and described in Chapter 5) of the highest possible reliability. Reliability, it will be remembered from Chapter 2, refers to the consistency over time of variables and to their internal consistency which is measured by the α coefficient. Thus the name of α analysis.

However, α factor analysis yields results little different from those of other methods and it is a matter of dispute whether the gains in the reliability of factor scores are of substantive value (see Cattell 1978). In brief there seems to be little advantage in α analysis compared with more conventional methods.

Significance of factor loadings

Regardless of what method of condensation is used it is necessary to know whether a factor loading is significant or not. There are various methods for computing the significance of loadings which will be briefly discussed.

A factor loading of 0.3 indicates that 9 per cent of the variance is accounted for by the factor. This is taken as large enough to indicate that the loading is salient. Thus in factor analyses where the sample is at least 100 subjects this is a reasonable criterion. Loadings of 0.3 or larger are regarded as significant. However, many factor analysts find this too rigorous. Cattell indeed regards loadings as low as 0.15 as salient, although in my view this can lead to problems of replication.

It was shown in Chapter 3 that factor loadings are correlations. The statistical significance of correlations is given in tables in most large statistical texts. If we adopt the 0.01 level of significance (see Chapter 2) we can take this as the criterion for regarding factor loadings as significant. With a large sample of 300 or more loadings as small as 0.15 become salient. However, these account for a very small percentage of variance – just over 2 per cent which is not impressive.

This method fails to take account of the number of variables in the analysis and the number of factors. As has been shown, as factors emerge from the analysis they get smaller and are also inflated by unique variance. This means that more rigorous criteria should be used for later factors. However, the rationale of such corrections is ingenious but essentially arbitrary.

In brief, I prefer to adopt the first approach: to regard as salient loadings above 0.3. However, if in large samples I obtain a loading of 0.298, I would not regard this as worthless.

Finally it should be noted that in practice I would not be considering the significance of factor loadings after the first stage of factor analysis but only after the factors had been rotated, a procedure to be discussed in the next chapter.

SUMMARY AND CONCLUSIONS

1 Common, specific and error variance were defined.
2 Unique variance was defined as specific plus error variance.
3 In principal components analysis error and specific variance are not separate.
4 In factor analysis specific and error variance may be separated by the insertion of communalities of less than 1 in the diagonals of the correlation matrix.
5 Factors may be further distinguished from components because factors are hypothetical, but estimated from actual variables, whereas components are real accounting for the variance in a particular matrix. The factor loadings of principal components are the correlations with actual combinations of variables.
6 Principal components is one method of condensing a matrix of correlations or reducing its rank.
7 Other methods have been developed to yield common factors and to separate specific from error variance.
8 Principal factors or principal axes is one such method. It is identical to principal components but communalities of less than 1 are put in the diagonals of the correlation matrix, thus, in principle, eliminating error variance.
9 Estimation of the diagonal entries has caused a severe problem in factor analysis. This is especially important because the communalities affect the results.
10 Associated with this is the problem of the number of factors to extract. However, these two problems are intertwined.

11 Various solutions to this problem have been developed.
  (a) Thurstone's iterative method for computing communalities. This, however, has to assume that the number of factors emerging from the first iteration is correct.
  (b) SMCs can be calculated but these can lead to communalities greater than unity and factorizations using this method do not always reproduce known factors.
  (c) Thurstone developed a statistical method for extracting significant factors but this appears to be too lenient.
  (d) Minimum residual methods have been used which calculate factors without using the diagonals. However, the more efficient multiple method works only when the number of factors is known. Furthermore these methods can give misleading solutions and communalities larger than 1.
12 Maximum likelihood factor analysis has a statistical test for the correct number of factors and is thus a preferred method for many analysts. However, it is computationally complex and in large matrices when reliable variables are used it produces results only trivially different from the more simple solutions. The main use of this method is in confirmatory analysis.
13 α factor analysis attempts to maximize the reliability of factor scores but otherwise gives results little different from those of principal factors.
14 Image analysis is brilliantly ingenious but it has problems concerning the use of specific variance, the meaning of the factor loadings and the fact that generally the results are little different from those more conventional solutions.
15 Finally the salience and significance of factor loadings was discussed and an arbitrary and conservative criterion of 0.3 was shown to be useful.

CONCLUSIONS

From this discussion some conclusions may be drawn. In general all these methods of condensation give remarkably similar results, although Cattell (1978) has shown that the choice of the number of factors to extract and to a lesser extent the communalities to be inserted in the diagonals of the correlation matrix are critical to obtaining sound replicable factors. In general principal factor analysis is an adequate method especially if the communalities inserted are those found in minimum residual solutions. Maximum likelihood factor analysis is also a good technique for initial condensation, with the advantage that there is a statistical test for the number of factors. Similarly principal components analysis, despite the fact that components are real rather than hypothetical factors, gives results closely similar to both principal factors and maximum likelihood methods.

However, even if the initial condensation has been completed, the task of the factor analyst is not finished. It was seen with principal components analysis that as an artefact of the algebra a general factor first emerged followed by bipolar factors, i.e. factors with high positive and negative loadings. Furthermore factors with many loadings are hard to interpret and understand. Ideally some method is needed to simplify factors and for this purpose rotation of factors has been developed. Factor rotation is essential for adequate factor analyses and this together with other essentials for good factor analyses are the subject of our next chapter.

Chapter 5

Rotation of factors

Chapter 4 was concerned with different methods of condensing a matrix of correlations and their comparison with principal components analysis. However, as was discussed in that chapter, even after factor analysis has been completed, by whatever method, factors have to be rotated before they can be interpreted. In principal components, for example, it an is artefact of the method that a general factor is produced followed by a series of bipolar factors. Thus interpretation of these components as reflecting anything but their algebra is dubious.

As was argued in the last chapter, factor analysis can be seen as reducing the ranks of a matrix. Thus on rare occasions it might be useful simply to demonstrate that a given number of factors would explain the variance, regardless of what these were. If this is so, then the unrotated factor solution can be left as it is. However, as was demonstrated in Chapter 1, in psychology and the social sciences the aim of factor analysis is to explain and account for the observed correlations and this means that the factors must be interpreted and identified. For this unrotated solutions are not useful.

This is not only because factors with many large loadings are hard to identify, and the loadings reflect the algebra by which they were computed, but also because there is no one perfect or ideal solution in factor analysis, as will be shown below. Indeed there is almost an infinity of mathematically equivalent sets of factors.

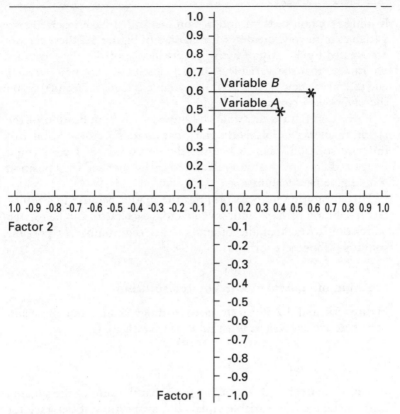

Figure 5.1 Factor loadings

THE GEOMETRIC PICTURE OF FACTOR ANALYSIS

I have not discussed the geometric approach to factor analysis in this *Easy Guide* because modern factor analyses are carried out by computers using matrix algebra, and it is more helpful therefore to try to explicate the algebra. Nevertheless the geometry of factor analysis can be revealing and an excellent account is to be found in Thomson (1954).

Factors can be represented in Euclidean space and Figure 5.1 illustrates two factors and the factor loading of two variables. As can be seen variable *A* loads 0.5 on factor 1 and 0.4 on factor 2 and *B* loads 0.6 on factor 1 and 0.6 on factor 2. Variables can fall in any of the four quadrants. For example, we could have a variable loading −0.8 on factor 1 and 0.2 on factor 2. I have inserted two variables in the one quadrant for clarity. In Figure 5.2 these factors are rotated by 30°. By drawing perpendiculars from the new axes we can see that the variable A now loads 0.6 on the new factor 1 and 0.2 on the new factor 2, while variable B loads 0.76 and 0.36 on the same two factors.

These two figures illustrate the meaning and implication of the claim, made earlier in this chapter, that there is a virtual infinity of different solutions. This is because these two axes or factors could be rotated into any position relative to each other and each position would give new loadings.

This illustration in fact simplifies the matter because in a multi-factor solution perhaps with seven factors each factor can be rotated in relation to each of the others so that the number of possible solutions is indeed enormous.

Meaning of equivalence in rotated solutions

Figures 5.1 and 5.2 illustrate how loadings change but the claim that these are equivalent must now be investigated.

Variance explained

It will be remembered from Chapter 3 that the sum of the squared factor loadings of a variable equals the proportion of variance for that variable explained by the factors.

Variable A
  Variance explained by Figure 5.1, $0.25 + 0.16 = 41\%$
  Variance explained by Figure 5.2, $0.36 + 0.04 = 40\%$

Variable B
  Variance explained by Figure 5.1, $0.36 + 0.36 = 72\%$
  Variance explained by Figure 5.2, $0.58 + 0.13 = 71\%$

Thus it can be seen that in terms of variance explained within the rounding errors of these rough diagrams the rotated and original solutions are the same.

Several points should be noted about this rotation.

1 The diagonals OA for test A and OB for test B each remain the same length after the rotations. These may be thought of as the test vectors, **A** and **B**, located in factor space by loadings on the two factors.

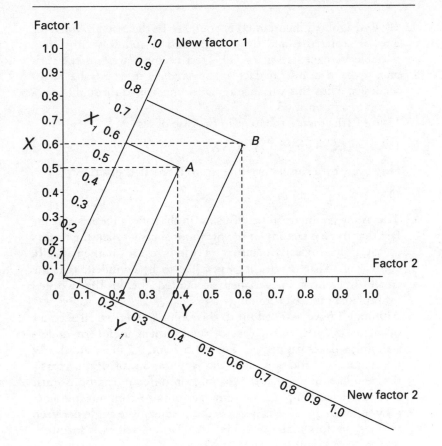

	Factor 1	Factor 2
Variable A		
Unrotated	0.5	0.4
Rotated	0.6	0.2
Variable B		
Unrotated	0.6	0.6
Rotated	0.76	0.36

Figure 5.2 Rotated factor loadings

2 By Pythagoras's theorem (1) is bound to be the case provided the axes are rotated round their origin and *A* and *B* or any other variables remain stationary. This test vector represents the variance explained by the factors, located as it is by the factor loadings. Thus this variance remains unchanged throughout rotation to any position.

3 Using Pythagoras's theorem in the case of test A:

$$OA^2 = OX^2 + OY^2 \, (OY = AX).$$

However, by a similar argument, in the rotated position

$$OA^2 = OX_1{}^2 + OY_1{}^2.$$

This is the geometrical proof using Pythagoras's theorem of the fact that rotated factors, in the orthogonal case (when the factors are at right angles), in terms of variance are mathematically equivalent. That is why it is possible to be confident that the small differences in variance accounted for in the worked examples are indeed rounding errors.

4 Although I have avoided up to this point a geometrical account of factor analysis, in the case of rotation it is useful for understanding what is happening. Figures 5.1 and 5.2 illustrate clearly the nature of rotation and the application of Pythagoras's theorem has shown that the loadings in different rotations must be equivalent. Simple trigonometry can also compute the new rotated loadings. This is because the cosine of the angle between two test vectors represents their correlation. The two formulae required are as follows

$$OX_1 = F_1 \cos \theta + F_2 \sin \theta \qquad (5.1)$$

where F_1 and F_2 are the initial loadings and θ is the angle of rotation.

$$OY_1 = F_2 \cos \theta - F_1 \sin \theta \qquad (5.2)$$

In our example, $\theta = 30°$; therefore $\cos 30° = 0.866$ and $\sin 30° = 0.5$. Thus from formula (5.1)

$$OX_1 = 0.5 \times 0.866 + 0.4 \times 0.5 = 0.43 + 0.20 = 0.63.$$

From formula (5.2)

$$OY_1 = 0.4 \times 0.866 - 0.5 \times 0.5 = 0.35 - 0.25 = 0.10.$$

These differences from the graphical solution are due to the roughness of the graph. Note however that this solution accounts for 40 per cent of the variance of A, as did the original solution.

Thus

$0.5^2 + 0.4^2 = 0.25 + 0.16 = 41\%$ of the variance (original).
$0.63^2 + 0.1^2 = 0.397 + 0.01 = 40.7\%$.

Conclusions concerning rotations

From the simple example of rotation illustrated in Figures 5.1 and 5.2 it is clear that rotating factors changes the factor loadings and thus the meaning of the factors, but that the different factor analytic solutions are mathematically equivalent in that they explain the same amount of variance in each variable and thus in the matrix as a whole. Furthermore the rotated factors reproduce the original correlations precisely as well as the unrotated solution.

However, it is equally clear that the rotated factors may take up any position in factor space and that accordingly, as has been argued, there is a virtual infinity of solutions. Since, as has been seen, these are mathematically equivalent, there is no mathematical reason for choosing one rather than another, which is precisely why the results of the first condensation, by whatever method, should not be interpreted as the final solution. In this chapter, therefore, it will be necessary to discuss how one solution is chosen from the array of possible rotations. Before this is done, however, a few other points must be clarified.

Reproducing the original correlations

It will be remembered that one of the tests of a factor analysis was its ability to reproduce the original correlation matrix. Thus if rotated factors are indeed equivalent we should expect the factor loadings of Figure 5.1 to yield the same correlation between variables A and B as do the rotated loadings in Figure 5.2. I shall illustrate this equivalence by computing the correlations from the two sets of loadings. The formula for computing the correlation is $r_{xy} = r_{x1y1} + r_{x2y2}$ where r_{xy} is the correlation between variables x and y; r_{x1y1} is the factor loading of variables x and y on factor 1; r_{x2y2} is the factor loading of variables x and y on factor 2. We can apply this formula to the factor loadings in Figures 5.1 and 5.2:

$r_{ab} = 0.5 \times 0.6 + 0.4 \times 0.6 = 0.54$ from loadings in Figure 5.1

$r_{ab} = 0.6 \times 0.76 + 0.2 \times 0.36 = 0.53$ from loadings in Figure 5.2.

Clearly these are the same within rounding errors. Thus the rotated factors are as good at explaining the common variance, the correlations, as the original solution. This is further evidence of the mathematical equivalence of different rotations.

Graphical rotations   It is possible to carry out rotations by the graphical methods described above. Indeed in the early days of factor analysis factors were rotated graphically. However, when there is a large number of factors it is a tedious and lengthy process. For this reason mathematical analytic methods of rotation have been developed in which the calculations can be performed by computer. These will be briefly described later in this section. Before this a distinction must be made between orthogonal and oblique rotations.

Orthogonal rotations   In orthogonal rotations the factors are rotated such that they are always at right angles to each other. This means that the factors are uncorrelated (cos 90° = 0). As Cattell (1978) has argued, in searching for factors which are fundamental dimensions for understanding psychological phenomena it is unlikely, *a priori*, that factors would be uncorrelated. In personality, for example, where there are environmental and genetic determinants at work, it would be most surprising to find orthogonal factors.

Oblique rotations   In oblique rotations the factor axes can take up any position in factor space, hence the name. The cosine of the angle between the factor axes indicates the correlation between them. Oblique rotation of factors allows more freedom in selecting the position of factors in factor space than does orthogonal rotation where there is the constraint of orthogonality. What positions should be selected and on what criteria will be discussed later in this chapter. As will be shown, rotation is the critical issue in the use of factor analysis in psychology and the other social sciences.

Problems with oblique rotations   Nunnally (1978) points out a number of problems with oblique rotations which should be borne in mind when interpreting the results. These are set out below.

1 The sum of squared loadings in any row would equal h^2 only by

chance. Thus oblique loadings do not clearly indicate the proportion of variance for each variable explained by the factors.
2 Similarly, only by chance does the sum of squares of the factor loadings in the columns equal the total variance in the matrix.
3 Finally the original correlations between the variables cannot be reproduced from the cross products of the factor loadings.

These statistical losses have to be set against the logical advantages of oblique analysis, namely that the axes can take up any position and that in the real world it is unlikely that important determinants of scores on ability and personality tests are orthogonal.

Factor structure   The factor structure consists of the correlations of the original variables with the rotated factors. The factor structure loadings of a rotated factor analysis are the equivalent of the factor loadings in the unrotated factor matrix (as has been shown in this chapter).

Factor pattern   The factor pattern consists of weights which are mainly useful for determining factor scores, the scores of subjects on the factors. Factor scores will be discussed later in this chapter. The factor pattern matrix usually closely resembles the structure matrix and is often used in research reports as if the elements were correlations with the variables. This can be misleading when the factors are highly correlated.

In orthogonal rotations the factor pattern and the factor structure are identical. In oblique rotations this is not the case and it is important, as has been argued above, that the structure and not the pattern is interpreted.

Reference vector structure   In oblique rotations a reference vector structure is used, for ease of computation, which consists of axes which are 90° to the oblique factors running through a cluster of variables. Many factor analysts simply regard such a reference vector structure as the oblique structure matrix, and some analytic computer programs print this out as the structure matrix. Nunnally (1978) argues that this use of the reference vector structure can be misleading in that it provides an apparent simplification which is difficult to interpret. The more correlated the factors the more dissimilar are the structure matrix and the reference vector matrix.

Nevertheless, given modern computing there is no reason to use the reference vectors. The actual factors give the best representation of the variance.

Having examined these most important aspects of rotation and clarified the meanings of some of the terms, we are now in a position to discuss the critical feature of rotation: selecting the best position for the factor axes. As has been argued previously, and it cannot be emphasized too much, much of the scientific value of factor analyses depends on proper rotation. Without it, as Cattell (1978) has shown, results cannot be trusted. However, before this discussion a brief explanation of factor scores, mentioned in connection with the factor pattern, is necessary.

Factor scores

Factors, as has been seen, give the most parsimonious account of the variance in a correlation matrix. Factors, of course, are linear combinations of variables. Thus to score subjects on the factors makes good sense. Factor scores can be obtained in a number of ways. I shall describe here the most simple.

A simple method of estimating factor scores   Add together the scores on the variables which load most highly on the factor. This statistically crude method correlates highly, in most cases, with more elaborate procedures in which multiple regressions of all the variables on to the factors are computed. The pattern matrix may be used in these calculations which are fully described in Mulaik (1987).

SIMPLE STRUCTURE: THE BEST POSITION

As has been shown, all positions of the factor axes are mathematically equivalent and all explain the original correlation matrix equally well. However, there is a rational basis for choosing between them: the law of parsimony.

Thus each factor solution can be thought of as a hypothesis to account for the observed correlations in the correlation matrix. However, the law of parsimony, often referred to as Lloyd Morgan's canon or Occam's razor, states that we should pick the simplest explanation of those that fit the facts. This principle is regularly applied in the natural sciences where it has proved highly effective. On this basis, therefore, it makes sense to pick the most simple solution from the infinity of rotations. This is the rationale for rotation to simple structure.

Definition of simple structure

Thurstone (1947) was responsible for the criterion of simple structure for the rotation of factors. Thurstone proposed five criteria for deciding on simple structure, although two of these are of overriding importance, namely that each factor should have a few high loadings with the rest of the loadings being zero or close to zero. Thurstone's criteria were as follows.

1 Each row of the rotated matrix should contain at least one zero.
2 In each factor the minimum number of zero loadings should be the number of factors in the rotation.
3 For every pair of factors there should be variables with zero loadings on one and significant loadings on the other.
4 For every pair of factors a large proportion of the loadings should be zero, at least in a matrix with a large number of factors.
5 For every pair of factors there should be only a few variables with significant loadings on both factors.

Essentially, as can be seen, the criterion of simple structure is a factor matrix in which the factors each have a few high loadings. In modern factor analytic practice, as will be discussed, this is the aim, and many methods of obtaining simple structure attempt to maximize the number of zero or near zero loadings, hence the use of reference vectors. Certainly the strict Thurstonian approach is no longer followed.

Other advantages of simple structure

Cattell (1978), who has done much to modernize the original approach of Thurstone, has argued convincingly that there are other advantages to the attainment of simple structure beyond the fact that it is the most simple account.

1 Simple structure factors are usually simple to interpret because they have only a few high loadings.
2 Simple structure factors are replicable. This is highly important because, as must be obvious, factor analysis would be a worth-

less scientific procedure if the factors changed from study to study. Since there is a multiplicity of solutions in factor analysis replicability is a serious problem. Cattell (1978) has argued indeed that many controversies in factor analysis as to the number and nature of factors, e.g. in the fields of personality and ability, simply result from failure by analysts to reach simple structure. Kline and Barrett (1983) demonstrated that this was so with personality questionnaires.

This replicability of simple structure factors also extends to matrices where the tests or variables are not identical. Thus it would be a serious flaw if factors changed simply because different tests of a variable were used. Suffice it to say here that when simple structure is not attained such changeable factors are common.

Indeed some critics of factor analysis, such as Heim (1975), have attempted to write off factor analysis as a scientific technique simply because of the multiplicity of solutions and the problems of replicating the factors. However, these criticisms are now outmoded. If simple structure can be attained replicable factors can be extracted.

3 Simple structure rotations in studies of artificial matrices, where the determinants are known (often referred to as plasmodes), yield factors which closely resemble them. This gives further confidence that simple structure factors are the best solution to the problems of rotation.

Conclusions concerning simple structure

Simple structure rotations yield interpretable, replicable factors which resemble the real factors in matrices where these are known. For these reasons I am in full agreement with Cattell and all serious workers in factor analysis that the attainment of simple structure is essential to factor analysis. Where this has not been done there is little reason to take the results seriously. However, it should be noted that the simplicity of oblique rotations may refer to the reference vectors, not the actual factors.

How is simple structure to be obtained? So far in this chapter I have demonstrated in a simple example how rotations are carried out, graphically and using simple geometric and trigonometric principles. It has been demonstrated that all orthogonal rotations are mathematically equivalent and it has been argued that the simplest solution should be chosen on logical and empirical grounds. However, it was also argued that many factor analyses failed to reach simple structure. Cattell (1978) has demonstrated that this failure is due to a number of different defects in carrying out the analysis. In fact Cattell (1978) proposed a set of rules for carrying out adequate factor analyses which would overcome these defects and allow simple structure to be obtained. Before these rules are scrutinized, however, it is necessary to discuss rotations a little further because poor rotation is perhaps the most important cause of failing to reach simple structure.

Simple structure rotations

It should be obvious that graphical rotation by hand, where many factors are involved, is a long and tedious process. To rotate the axes to all the possible positions relative to each other in order to select the most simple position is more work than most investigators would have time for. Similarly the algebraic calculations involved in rotations to all possible positions are lengthy and exceedingly wasteful of computer space and time, especially with large matrices.

For all these reasons analytic algebraic solutions have been developed and it is these which are used in the computer programs for rotated factor analysis. However, not all are equally efficient at attaining simple structure and it is necessary to discuss these albeit briefly.

Analytic programs

Analytic rotation methods aim to specify in mathematical terms the essentials of Thurstone's simple structure. Thus the computer program instantiating these procedures should rotate the factors to a simple structure position, as distinct from the mathematics described earlier in this chapter which simply rotates factors. I shall deal first with orthogonal rotations.

Varimax (Kaiser 1958)

This aims at simple structure while keeping the factor axes orthogonal. As has been explained, this means that the rotated factors are uncorrelated and the communalities and the ability to reproduce the original correlation matrix are identical to the original factor analysis. Although in some instances simple structure cannot be obtained with orthogonal factors, where this is possible it is generally agreed that Varimax is the most efficient procedure.

Varimax aims to maximize the sum of *variances* of squared loadings in the columns of the factor matrix. This produces in each column (which is, of course, a factor) loadings which are either high or near zero. This is one of the critical features of simple structure. A clever feature of Varimax, as Nunnally (1978) points out, is that the procedure is applied to the loadings squared rather than the actual loadings. As it removes the negative signs in the columns, this also removes the effects of such negatives on the variance, effects which are quite artificial since they depend on how a variable is scored. For example, if an extraversion test were to be scored for introversion there would be a perfect negative correlation between the two sets of scores and the signs of the factor loadings would be simply reversed.

The squared loadings of the rows are standardized by dividing them by the sum of squares in the row. This ensures that all variables have the same weight in the solution.

Certainly I have found that Varimax is an excellent method of reaching orthogonal simple structure and that in many case oblique solutions are virtually identical because the correlation between the factors is so small as to be negligible.

In conclusion, where an orthogonal simple structure rotation is desired, Varimax should be applied.

Oblique rotation programs

Oblique rotations are far more complex than orthogonal rotations because the factor axes can take up any position in factor space. There is a far larger number of possible programs from which to choose: Carroll, who has done much to produce efficient analytic simple structure oblique rotations, has three – Quartmin, Oblimin and Biquartmin. Others are Oblimax, Covarimin, Binormamin and Promax, which was developed in Great Britain. Direct Oblimin is another example. The mathematics of these methods is fully described by Gorsuch (1983), who actually explicates nineteen rotational procedures (which he claims is only a sample), so I shall restrict myself to a few comments here which are important for interpreting the factors.

Earlier in this chapter we described the three terms: factor structure, factor pattern and reference vector factors. It was noted that in the orthogonal case the factor pattern (the weights on the variables to produce factor scores) and the factor structure (correlations between the variables and factors) are identical. However, in the oblique case this is no longer so.

With oblique rotations it was also noted that there is a reference vector structure which is sometimes reported as if it were the factor structure and it is necessary to discuss this a little further.

The reference vector structure

In oblique rotations if a factor axis is placed through a cluster of variables and a reference vector is then placed at 90° to this axis the loadings of these variables on the reference vector will be zero. By using a set of reference vectors orthogonal to the oblique factors it is possible quite easily to produce a set of simple structure reference vectors. If these are simple so is the factor pattern, but unfortunately the factor structure itself (the correlations of the variables and factors) is not necessarily so simple if the factors are highly correlated. Figure 5.3 shows a reference vector and an oblique factor, illustrating how by putting a factor through clusters of variables zero loadings are obtained on the reference vectors. Thurstone (working on simple adding machines) employed this method and, as Loehlin (1987) points out, it is sometimes used in more modern computer programs. Figure 5.3 indicates that in orthogonal rotations the reference vectors would be identical to the factors because the factors are kept at right angles to each other. Thus simplifying the reference vector loadings also simplifies the actual factor loadings.

Finally it should be pointed out again that the simplicity of the reference vector structure is shared by the factor pattern, which consists of the weights to be used for the production of factor scores which will be discussed later in this chapter. As I have argued, following Nunnally (1978), the factor pattern is more difficult to interpret than the factor structure and certainly has not the same meaning. However, despite these problems it must be said that reference vectors and patterns are reported (see, for example, Loehlin 1987), and Child (1990) advocates their use. Some computer programs, indeed, as has been pointed out, print out the reference vector structure as the factor structure.

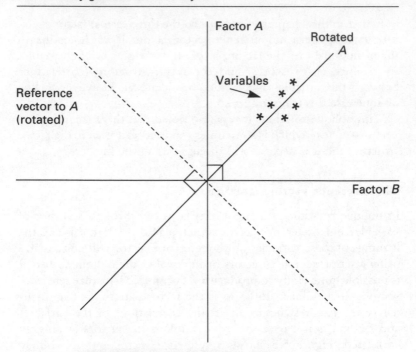

Figure 5.3 A reference vector in oblique rotation

Conclusions

This discussion of factor structures, patterns and reference vector structures has one clear conclusion. At least be certain which of these is being discussed and bear in mind its particular nature.

With this distinction between the three sets of results which can be obtained from oblique rotations we must now consider briefly a different approach to oblique rotation.

Maxplane and Rotoplot

Cattell (e.g. 1978) has developed what he calls topological programs for computing oblique rotations. Maxplane attempts to emulate the human eye in graphical rotations. This is done by maximizing the zero loadings on the reference vectors, achieved by putting these through clusters of variables. Cattell sets hyperplanes around these reference vectors which allow low loadings, say 0.05 and lower, to be regarded as zeros. The position which maximizes the hyperplane count (number of variables within the hyperplanes of the reference vectors) is regarded as simple structure. This criterion accounts for the name of the method. This program is the best instantiation in computer programs of the original Thurstonian approach.

Rotoplot is a program which presents on the screen the axes and their loadings from any automatic rotation program and allows the user to adjust these by eye as in the original graphical rotations. Cattell has always claimed that by these methods it is possible to 'polish' the results of any oblique rotation by computer program, even including Maxplane, and thus end up with a more simple structure. However, it has to be said that only Cattell and his colleagues use Maxplane and Rotoplot and that Rotoplot needs considerable skill and patience to use. Indeed the present writer has found it extremely difficult to make noticeable improvements on analytic rotations, although I have not the experience of Cattell with this technique. Incidentally, it is easy to make them worse with Rotoplot.

How should oblique rotations be carried out? I hope that readers are not too confused at this point. To summarize the position there are many different programs claiming to be able to rotate oblique factors to simple structure. In addition there is the difficulty of having three matrices of pattern loadings, structure loadings and reference vector loadings.

Fortunately this problem has been eased by studies of the relative efficiency of these programs at obtaining simple structure where the factors are previously known. Hakstian (1971) showed that Direct Oblimin and Maxplane were the two most effective methods for obtaining simple structure, but that Direct Oblimin was the more reliable because occasionally Maxplane could be caught out by certain clusters of variables and could give a misleading result. While the skilled user might notice this and use Rotoplot to correct the flaw, for most work Direct Oblimin is to be recommended. Actually it is a good check to use one other method of rotation, since any one method can be caught out occasionally by particular configurations of data. In most instances, however, there will not be considerable differences. If orthogonal simple structure is preferred then all authorities agree that Varimax is the most effective procedure.

This discussion of rotation was undertaken because it was argued in this chapter that simple structure must be obtained in factor analysis – because only then are the results replicable and likely to reflect determinants in the real world – and that good rotation is essential for simple structure. However, no matter how efficient the rotation at simplifying the factor matrix, if other criteria are not met simple structure will not be reached. Cattell and Kline (1977) have discussed the technical demands of adequate factor analyses (without which simple structure is impossible) and these will now be set out. These can be dealt with relatively briefly because most of the points have been dealt with in this and previous chapters on principal components and other factor analytic methods.

Technical rules for simple structure factor analyses

It should be noted that although these rules were first formulated by Cattell most reputable factorists would agree with them. Where Cattell is somewhat idiosyncratic this will be pointed out.

Sampling variables

In exploratory factor analysis the aim is to map the whole field. To do this, however, the full range of variables must be sampled. For example, no matter how perfect the rotation, if in an exploratory factor analysis of abilities no measures of mathematical ability were included, there could be no mathematical factor.

This point requires a little further elaboration. We distinguished specific and common factors. A specific factor was one that loaded only on one variable. Thus clearly to mark a factor at least three variables are required. Certainly one is insufficient.

All this means that in any field there must be a good rationale for sampling variables.

Sampling subjects

The factors emerging from factor analyses are affected by the samples from whom they are obtained. There are two problems here, which lead to different formulations of practice.

One argument indicates that samples should be homogeneous. For example, if we factored abilities and measures of academic success among a homogeneous sample of those with first class honours at Oxford and Cambridge, it is likely that intelligence would not load on academic success to any great degree. This is because this sample is homogeneous for intelligence. All are sufficiently intelligent to do well academically so that intelligence is not important in determining academic success compared with interest and flair at the particular subject. However, if we were to carry out a similar study using the whole range of IQ, intelligence would load highly on the academic success factor.

From this it might be concluded that heterogeneous samples should always be used. Homogeneous samples, by definition, lower variance and thus, as the algebra makes clear, lower factor loadings. In exploratory factor analyses, therefore, generally it is best to use heterogeneous samples and increase the variance.

However, there is another aspect to this argument which leads to a different conclusion. It can be argued that scores from different groups should not be added together. For example, if we studied two groups one with a mean IQ of 120 and the other with a mean IQ of 60, to add them together and factor their scores would appear nonsensical since the average IQ of these groups (given the same number in each) would not reflect any member of the group.

From this it might be concluded that only homogeneous groups should be factored. However, given the first argument this is not so. Certainly the two IQ groups should not be mixed but this is because such a sample does not reflect any real population. It is an unrepresentative sample.

Thus it should be concluded that heterogeneous and properly sampled groups should be used in factor analysis. Since it is not impossible that there are important differences between special groups, where this is suspected the factor structure should be checked in the relevant groups.

Sample size

Samples must not only be representative but must be of sufficient size to produce reliable factors. Guilford (1956) argued that 200 was a minimum figure but in my experience this is pessimistic. In data with a clear factor structure samples of 100 were quite sufficient. If factor analyses are carried out with samples smaller than these all results need replication in other samples. The rule is the more subjects the better.

Variable to subject ratio

For algebraic reasons it is essential that there are more subjects than variables. Where this is not the case the results are not meaningful. There have been various claims made concerning the ratio of subjects to variables running from as large as 10:1 as the necessary minimum down to 2:1. In my experience large factors emerge with clarity with samples with ratios of 2:1. Again the rule here is the bigger the ratio the better.

It should be noted that a study by Arrindel and van der Ende (1985) claimed that this ratio was less important than the ratio of subjects to factors. This should be more than 20:1. This is not as useful as might be thought in exploratory studies where one does not know how many factors will emerge. It might be a useful check, however.

Method of factor analysis

As Chapters 3 and 4 made clear, with large matrices the differences between these methods are usually small. Principal factor analysis seems to be a sensible choice, although some may prefer the statistical elegance of maximum likelihood methods where the number of factors to be extracted has a significance test.

Communalities to be placed in the factor analysis

The placing of communalities in the factor analysis, as has been seen, is important. Communalities of unity as in principal components analysis ensure that all the variance, including error variance, is included in the factors. The best estimate of communalities is probably that from the minimum residual analysis which was discussed in Chapter 4.

Number of factors to be rotated

There is no doubt that attaining simple structure depends closely on the number of factors which are rotated. Cattell (1978) has shown that rotation of too few factors tends to produce second–order factors. Second-order factors, which will be discussed towards the end of this chapter, are factors which emerge from the factor analysis of the correlations of the oblique factors. In effect second-order factors are broad, often too broad to be useful in interpretation. An example of second-order factors comes from the analysis of the correlations between personality test items. Usually there are a large number of correlated factors. Further analysis of these first-order or primary factors reveals usually four or five second-order factors which account for much of the variance in the items. The two largest of these are anxiety and extraversion – broad personality factors (see Kline 1993).

Thus if too few factors are rotated broad second-order factors emerge. If, however, too many factors are rotated then the factors split up.

Most computer packages have a default solution to this problem. They rotate factors with eigenvalues greater than 1. However, it has been shown by Cattell (1978) that in large matrices this greatly overestimates the number of factors.

There is now agreement among most factor analysts of any repute that Cattell's Scree test is just about the best solution to selecting the correct number of factors. Although Cattell attempts to give a statistical rationale for this procedure it is essentially a convenient algorithm which has been shown in artificial matrices to give the correct number of factors. Figure 5.4 shows a typical Scree test. In the Scree test a graph is made of the eigenvalues and the principal components. The cutoff point for factor rotation is where the line changes slope. In the case in Figure 5.4 five factors would be rotated. It is to be noted that the Scree test must be performed on principal components. Then principal factor analysis is performed and the factors selected by the Scree test are rotated.

One objection to the Scree test is that it is subjective. However, with practice there is usually high inter-scorer reliability. Where there is disagreement it is obviously sensible to compare the Scree test with some other method, perhaps the eigenvalues greater than one rule.

Another possibility is to use maximum likelihood factor analysis and use a statistical test to select the number of factors. Recently, in fact, with the cost of high speed computing falling many factor analysts are using maximum likelihood factor analysis and rotating the significant factors. Generally there is close agreement between these two techniques.

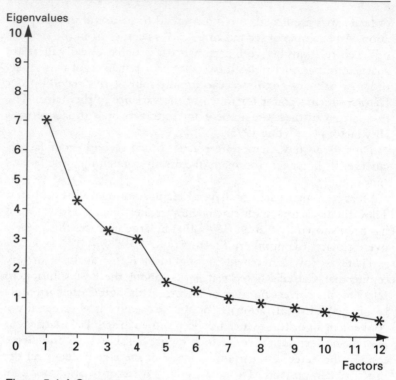

Figure 5.4 A Scree test

Choice of rotation

The choice of rotation has already been fully discussed in a previous section. If an orthogonal solution yields simple structure, as it frequently does, the Varimax rotation package is the one to choose. If the orthogonal rotation is simple it has the advantage that the factor loadings are equivalent to the original analysis and that we are dealing with the actual factors.

If an oblique rotation gives a better simple structure then the Direct Oblimin package is the one to choose. Remember that the factor pattern loadings are weights for estimating factor scores and that reference vectors maximizing the zero loadings in the matrix could differ considerably from the factors running through the clusters of variables.

Check factors against previous results

Factors can be checked against previous results statistically by a measure of factor similarity, which can be found in Cattell (1978), but this is only applicable where exactly the same set of variables has been used. Equally useful is to compare the interpretations of the factors. Although this is subjective, it is a simple enough task to make a convincing case that the factors are the same from study to study.

Check second-order factors

If sets of primary factors truly are equivalent then their second-order factors (resulting from the correlations between the factors) should be the same. Clearly second-order factors can only be computed where the primary factors are oblique.

Second-order factors are important in many applications of factor analysis in psychology. The main ability and personality factors are second order and it should be remembered that these are simply derived from the factor analysis of the correlations between factors. These factors therefore load initially on the first-order factors. This is why they are broad variables and why they are often of more psychological significance than the narrower primary factors.

This almost concludes our discussion of exploratory factor analysis. Before ending it I want briefly to discuss some factor analytic designs which are useful in applied psychology.

R analysis

R stands for regular factor analysis, as has so far been described in the *Easy Guide*. In R analysis the correlations between variables are factored and the factors account for individual differences between people. From R analysis have come the clearest psychometric findings – extraversion, fluid and crystallized intelligence and anxiety, to name the best known factors.

P analysis

In P analysis the traits within one individual are correlated and factored. P factors are unique to an individual. Many repeated measurements are necessary to compute the correlations and it has been rarely used.

Q analysis

In Q analysis the correlations between people rather than variables are factored. The normal data matrix is turned on its side. In this analysis the ratio of tests to subjects should be at least 2:1, so that if large samples are used considerable testing is necessary. Q factors load on individuals rather than tests and it is useful where classification into groups is required, as in diagnostic studies for example.

O analysis

In O analysis the scores of the same subjects on different occasions are factored. If measures of processes such as psychotherapy and education, together with measures of environmental events, are included in the analyses some determinants of change might be revealed.

Finally two other techniques have been described by Cattell (1978): S analysis, where the responses of two people on several occasions are measured; and T analysis, in which the test-retest reliabilities of tests are factored. These have been rarely used.

The use of these somewhat abstruse modes of factor analysis is not recommended until one has had considerable experience with the R technique.

SUMMARY AND CONCLUSIONS

In this chapter the problem of the equivalence of factors rotated to different positions has been faced. A number of points have been made.

1 The mathematical equivalence of rotated and initial factors is demonstrated.
2 It is shown that simple structure factors are replicable and interpretable.
3 It is demonstrated that simple structure can be reached provided that certain technical criteria are met in the factor analysis, of which the most important are
   (a) good sampling of variables;

(b) good sampling of subjects;

(c) large samples, with 100 subjects as the minimum;

(d) a ratio of subjects to variables of at least 2:1;

(e) the use of principal or maximum likelihood factor analysis;

(f) the use of a Scree test or statistical test to obtain the number of factors;

(g) the use of Varimax rotation or, if oblique, Direct Oblimin rotation.

4 As regards interpretation in the oblique case, it is shown that one should be aware of the differences between factor patterns, factor structure and reference vectors.

5 Finally second-order factors and other types of factor analysis are described.

Chapter 6

Confirmatory factor analysis and path analysis

Although confirmatory analysis has been mentioned in our discussion of factor analysis, so far I have concentrated upon the explication of exploratory analysis, as this is by far the most widely used. However, many psychologists believe that confirmatory factor analysis is in principle a superior method to exploratory analysis because it tests hypotheses, which is fundamental to the scientific method.

When confirmatory analysis is discussed it usually refers to the maximum likelihood method of analysis (briefly mentioned in Chapter 4) used to test an hypothesized factor structure. This method, together with a whole set of mathematical techniques designed to test various different models, has been instantiated in a computer program known as LISREL (Joreskog and Sorbom 1984). In this chapter I shall discuss only briefly the model testing aspects of the relationships between factors (referred to in LISREL as the structural model). Rather I shall concentrate on confirmatory analysis which is part of the measurement model which deals with the relationships between observed variables and factors (latent variables).

Confirmatory factor analysis is highly complex algebraically, and LISREL or an equivalent program would always be used for any computations. However, confirmatory analysis compares models which path analysis handles quite clearly and it can be understood in principle from this technique. I shall therefore set out below some of the basic formulations of path analysis.

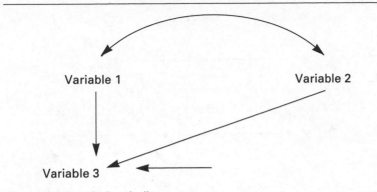

Figure 6.1 A typical path diagram

PATH ANALYSIS

As Loehlin (1987) points out, path analysis, factor analysis and structural equation analysis (of which LISREL is an example) are all types of latent variable analysis, so called because some of the variables are not directly observed. In factor analysis the latent variables are, of course, factors. Loehlin (1987) is an excellent source of information on path analysis and latent variable analysis in general and readers who wish to know more than the simple account in this chapter should consult this book.

Path diagrams

Path diagrams represent the relationships between a number of variables. Figure 6.1 shows a typical path diagram, within which a straight one-headed arrow represents a causal relationship between the variables and a curved double-headed arrow represents a simple correlation between the variables.

In Figure 6.1 variable 3 might be a child's score on an anxiety test, and variables 1 and 2 the anxiety scores of the mother and father. These would be correlated because of the phenomenon of assortative mating: anxious people tend to marry other anxious people. The unlabelled arrow to variable 3 indicates that there are other influences on anxiety than those represented by variables 1 and 2. Such arrows are known as residual arrows, which are discussed later in this section. Notice that this path diagram is essentially a model because it is postulated that the anxiety level of the parents affects that of the child. If the curved arrow were omitted from

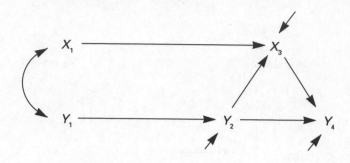

Figure 6.2 A path diagram involving time

variables 1 and 2 it would indicate that there was no correlation between the parents' anxiety levels and this would effectively represent another model. Figure 6.2 shows a path diagram in which time is involved. In this diagram the subscripts indicate times of measurement – in this case there are four; X is a variable measured on occasions 1 and 3; Y is a variable measured on occasions 2 and 4; and X and Y are correlated.

It can be seen from the figure that X_1 affects X_3 directly and Y_4 via X_3. Y_1 affects Y_2, Y_4 and X_3 directly. It also affects Y_4 indirectly. The unlabelled arrows at Y_2, X_3 and Y_4 indicate that there are some unspecified influences on Y_4. These are the residual arrows.

Classification of variables in path diagrams

Variables in path diagrams fall into one of the following two classes.

1 *Independent or source variables.* Independent variables are causally independent *vis-à-vis* other variables in the path diagram. They have no arrows directed towards them. Their connecting arrows are always outwards. They are the source of causation in the diagram.

2 *Dependent or downstream variables.* These are causally dependent on other variables in the path diagram. They have arrows directed towards them.

Further points about path diagrams

1 All source variables should be interconnected by curved arrows. If they are not it is assumed that the correlation is zero.
2 Downstream variables are never connected by curved arrows. If there are correlations between downstream variables (caused by variables not in the diagram) then these are indicated by curved arrows between the residual arrows.
3 Residual arrows point only at downstream variables.
4 Residual arrows should be attached to every downstream variable. If they are not it is assumed that all the variance is accounted for by the independent variables.
5 All significant causal connections between variables in a path diagram should be indicated by a direct arrow. Thus in Figure 6.2 it is assumed that Y_1 does not directly affect X_3.
6 It is assumed that the relationships indicated by arrows are linear.
7 It is possible to include in path diagrams causal loops and variables where each one influences the other. Thus, for example, time R spent reading might influence academic success A. However, academic success could well influence time spent reading. Thus in a path diagram A and R would be linked by two arrows, one pointing at A and the other at R. In a feedback loop each variable is linked by an arrow thus: A to B to C to A, A being the independent variable.

Such are the conventions of path diagrams which are essentially descriptive. However, working with empirical data these can be the subject of path analysis and this must be described.

Loehlin (1987) has an excellent summary of path analysis to which readers should refer. Here I shall set out the main points which will be useful for understanding the principles of confirmatory analysis. It is assumed that all variables are in standard score form (means of 0, standard deviations of 1) which simplifies the algebra. Raw scores can be used but with greater complications and they will not be explicated here.

1 In path analysis the correlation between any two variables equals the sum of the compound paths connecting these two points.
2 A compound path is defined as a path along arrows where there are (i) no loops, (ii) no going forward then backwards and (iii) one or no curved arrows for each path. It should be noted that it is possible to go backwards first and then forwards (allowing

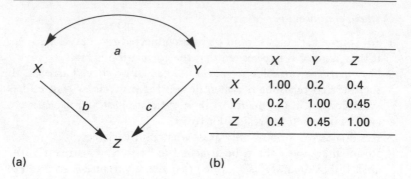

	X	Y	Z
X	1.00	0.2	0.4
Y	0.2	1.00	0.45
Z	0.4	0.45	1.00

(a)   (b)

Figure 6.3 A simple example of path analysis

events to be connected by cause). The forbidden path, however, would link events by consequence.

3 Since correlations between variables can be expressed as the sum of compound paths, this process can be reversed, and, given the correlations, the values of the causal paths can be solved.

Example of path analysis

I shall take the most simple example of path analysis to illustrate the algebra (Figure 6.3). Using the rules of path analysis the following calculations may be made.

$$r_{XY} = a$$
$$r_{XZ} = b + ac$$
$$r_{YZ} = c + ab.$$

From the correlation matrix values can be substituted in these equations:

$$a = 0.2$$
$$b + ac = 0.4$$
$$c + ab = 0.45.$$

Substituting 0.2 for a, these equations can be rewritten as

$$b + 0.2c = 0.4$$
$$c + 0.2b = 0.45.$$

Multiplying the second equation by 5 we obtain

$$b + 5c = 2.25.$$

Subtracting the first equation

$$b + 0.2c = 0.4$$

yields

$$4.8c = 1.85.$$

Thus $c = 0.385$. With $c = 0.385$ and $a = 0.2$ we can now solve for b. From $b + ac = 0.4$ we get

$$b + 0.385 \times 0.2 = 0.4 \qquad b + 0.077 = 0.4 \qquad b = 0.323.$$

From $c + ab = 0.45$ we get

$$0.385 + 0.2b = 0.45 \qquad 0.2b = 0.065 \qquad b = 0.325.$$

The difference is due to rounding error. Thus the paths $b = 0.32$ and $c = 0.39$ have been calculated. There are several points to be noted about these results.

1 With the correlations as observed and if the simple causal model is correct then it is possible to say that the causal influence of X on Z is 0.32 and of Y on Z is 0.39.
2 What do the path coefficients 0.32 and 0.39 mean? In fact they are partial regression coefficients (see Chapter 2). They indicate the extent to which a change in the variable at the tail of the arrow affects the variable at the head. That they are partial coefficients indicates that the changes occur with all other variables constant.
3 Standardized partial regression coefficients are β weights, the weights required to maximize the correlation between one variable and a set of other variables. This is the technique known as multiple regression (see Chapter 2). That they are β weights allows other important deductions to be made from path diagrams which may be seen as multiple regressions in diagrammatic form. Loehlin (1987), for example, points out one important deduction which may be made.
4 The predicted variance of Z from X and Y is the sum of the permitted paths from Z to itself from A or B or both. In Figure 6.3, the paths are X and back (b^2), Y and back (c^2), bac and cab. The variance explained by X and Y is therefore

$$0.32^2 + 0.39^2 + 2 \times (0.2 \times 0.32 \times 0.39) \qquad (cab = bac).$$

Thus the variance is 0.304. Thus 30 per cent of the variance in Z can be predicted from X and Y.

It is interesting to compare this multiple regression analysis through path diagrams with the standard regression formula:

$$R^2_{Z.XY} = \beta_1 r_{XZ} + \beta_2 r_{YZ}$$
$$= 0.4 \times 0.32 + 0.39 \times 0.45$$
$$= 0.304. \tag{6.1}$$

Latent variables, path analysis and confirmatory factor analysis

Where it is the case that all variables are measured, as in the examples in this chapter, it is possible to use these path analytic methods to solve for the β weights and investigate the variance accounted for in criterion variables. Sometimes, however, there are latent variables which cannot be measured directly and here the multiple regression approach will not work. Instead the simultaneous equations have to be solved using iterative methods or inserting numbers into the unknowns. Then an exact solution is not possible since no one solution will fit all the equations and then it is necessary to obtain the best fit.

A useful distinction should be made concerning the simultaneous equations in path diagrams. In the example of Figure 6.3 an exact solution was possible. This was because there were as many equations as unknowns. Such a path diagram is said to be just determined. Although a unique solution is possible, such path diagrams are not ideal in the scientific study of psychology or in the other social sciences. This is because, as was shown in our comparison of principal components and common factors, measures contain unique variance, comprising specific and error variance, and no solution which accounts for these could be generalizable. Incidentally, it should be pointed out at this juncture that a path diagram of a principal components analysis would be just determined.

In some cases, however, there are more equations than unknowns. Such path diagrams are overdetermined and no single solution can satisfy all the equations. What has to done is to select the solutions in which the path coefficients best account for the observed correlations. The fact that, in the overdetermined case, there is no exact solution, on the same arguments as were used above against just determined path diagrams, makes these path diagrams preferable. Given error and specific variance, an account

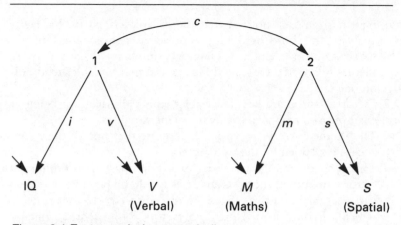

Figure 6.4 Factor analysis as a path diagram

which applied to the population could never fit perfectly any particular sample. This could only occur when all unique variance had been eliminated, i.e. when tests are perfectly valid.

There is a third case where there are fewer equations than variables. No unique solution is possible and these path diagrams are described as underdetermined. In these cases a sufficient number of the path coefficients have to be fixed so that the rest of the unknowns can be solved. This is usually done on the basis of previous research. However, this can only be effective in fields where there is reliable and accurate knowledge and this is not always the case. This problem will be discussed later in this section because it is crucial to the use of confirmatory analysis.

The precise mathematics of computing overdetermined simultaneous equations will not be discussed here, although the argument has been introduced at this point in the chapter because latent variables are the link between path analysis and factor analysis which, as I hope is now clear, deals with sets of latent variables which can account for observed variance and covariance. Now, as Loehlin (1987) points out, path models are ideal for representing the structures which confirmatory analysis puts to the statistical test.

Representation of a factor analysis in a path diagram

Figure 6.4 shows a path diagram of a factor analysis. The following notes should be made about the figures.

1 First it should be noticed that the data described in this factor analysis are those used in the principal components analysis worked out in Chapter 3. Here, for simplicity, I have assumed that there are two correlated factors and that variables load only on one factor.

2 Factors 1 and 2 are latent variables, this path diagram being an example of a path analysis using latent variables.

3 The residual arrows to variables indicate that not all their variance is explained by the two factors.

4 This path diagram is a model or a hypothesis concerning the factor structure of these variables. It would be possible to draw a path diagram of a three factor model, or a two factor model in which variables loaded on both factors. Note that a principal components model would have four factors, uncorrelated, and there would be no residual arrows, since principal components account for all the variance.

5 Thus path analysis can represent a factor analysis but there are as many path analyses as factor analytic solutions.

Figure 6.4 is more than an illustration of factor analysis. Using the path analytic rules and equations which were described earlier in this chapter, the path coefficients can be specified. Table 6.1 indicates the observed correlations and the path coefficients in Figure 6.4. From the path diagram of the factor analysis of the matrix reported in Chapter 3, it is clear that the correlations and factors can be specified according to the rules of path analysis.

Table 6.1 Observed correlations and path coefficients

r	Path	Variable	Factor pattern		Factor loadings	
			1	2	1	2
$r_{iv} = 0.4$	iv					
$r_{im} = 0.3$	icm	IQ	i	0	i	ic
$r_{is} = 0.2$	ics	V	v	0	v	vc
$r_{vm} = 0.2$	vcm	S	0	s	sc	s
$r_{vs} = 0.1$	vcs	M	0	m	mc	m
$r_{ms} = 0.3$	ms					

1 *The factor pattern*. The factor pattern represents the weights for predicting the factors. Thus they are the path coefficients as indicated. The 0s represent that there are no such paths between factor 1 and S and M or between factor 2 and IQ and V. The path

coefficients i, v, s and m are partial regression weights as was shown in an earlier section of this chapter.

2 *The factor structure.* This represents the correlations between the factors and the variables. In the oblique case these are not necessarily the same as the weights, as was shown in Chapter 5. In path analysis the correlation between variables is indicated by a permitted path.

Computing the path coefficients in Figure 6.4

In the path diagram in Figure 6.4, on which Table 6.1 is based, there are five unknowns: the paths i, v, m, s and c. However, as is shown in the table, there are six equations, and because there are more equations than unknowns an exact solution is not possible. This is the overdetermined case. However, a solution is possible through iterative methods, for which a computer program is essential and the principles of this solution are no different from those used in the solution of the path diagrams given earlier in this chapter.

Path diagrams in algebraic form

Path diagrams can be represented algebraically by structural equations and these must now be discussed. I shall clarify the nature of structural equations under a number of points.

1 Each equation expresses a downstream or dependent variable as a function of its causal paths.
2 There are therefore as many equations as downstream variables.
3 To construct a structural equation there must be a term for every straight arrow leading into the downstream variable. This term is the variable at the tail multiplied by its path coefficient.

An example of a structural equation

To illustrate the nature of structural equations I shall take the factor analysis discussed in Figure 6.4 and Table 6.1. The structural equations are

$$IQ = i_1 + R_{IQ}$$
$$V = v_1 + R_V$$
$$M = m_2 + R_M$$
$$S = s_2 + R_S$$

where the R is the residual arrow associated with IQ.

These structural equations are similar to the factor pattern loadings, as can be seen from Table 6.1. The structural equations also include the unique variance. The solutions of these equations are highly similar to those of the path coefficients and as is to be expected they are undetermined in this example.

Readers who would like a demonstration of the fact that path analyses and structural equations are identical are referred to Loehlin (1987) who shows their equivalence with a worked example.

So far in this chapter I have demonstrated that path diagrams are able to illustrate correlational and other relationships between variables and that path analysis enables these relationships to be quantified. It was shown that path coefficients are partial regression weights and that where all variables are observed these weights can be computed directly.

However, where latent variables are introduced, as in factor analysis, undetermined solutions have to be used and methods for calculating these are available in computer packages.

It was also shown that factor analyses can be represented in path diagrams and in path analyses and that these can be equivalently represented in structural equations. Each path diagram of a factor analysis is a model of how the variables are related (as, of course, is each factor analysis).

In the next section of this chapter I shall show how confirmatory analysis seeks to test which is the best fit to the data of these varied models.

The path diagram and confirmatory analysis

As has been argued, the factor analysis in Figure 6.4 is a hypothetical factor structure to account for the observed correlations: two correlated factors with loadings each on two variables and zero loadings on the others. This is a two factor simple structure hypothesis. Table 6.1 shows the corresponding path coefficients.

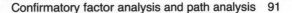

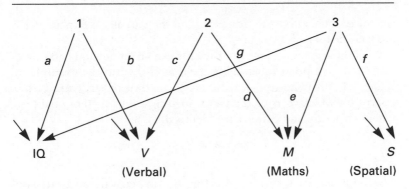

Figure 6.5 A three factor orthogonal solution

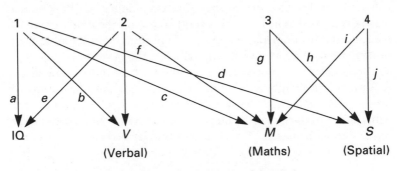

Figure 6.6 A principal components analysis of these data

Figure 6.5 shows a three factor orthogonal analysis of the same data. Using all the same path analytic rules we could develop a set of simultaneous equations in order to solve for the unknowns. Notice that the hypothesis in this path diagram is quite different from that of Figure 6.4. Thus it has three uncorrelated factors and factor 3 loads on the three variables IQ, maths and space. Factor two loads on verbal and mathematical ability. Actually, in view of what is known about human abilities, this is a most unlikely factor structure.

Figure 6.6 shows the principal component analysis of the data. This path diagram has several noteworthy features. First, it is clear that it is a principal components analysis because there are as many factors as variables and because there are no residual arrows. This lack of residual arrows indicates that all the variance is explained by the four factors.

In all these cases the path coefficients can be set out and computed using iterative procedures. This then, as shown in the example in Table 6.1, provides us with the factor pattern or structure in the case of oblique factors or the factor loadings in the orthogonal case where structure and pattern are identical.

Testing the solutions

The solutions are tested by inserting the solved values of the path coefficients into the original equations from which they were derived and comparing them with the observed correlations. Thus to take Table 6.1 as an example, for the correlation between IQ and intelligence we would put the solved values of i and v. These solved values are subtracted from the observed values and a residual matrix is formed. The larger this residual matrix the worse the fit of the solution. In confirmatory analysis, a number of different tests of fit have been developed to decide which is the best solution, but at this stage what is important is to see the logic of the argument.

With this description of path diagrams and the illustration of how it is possible by using simultaneous equations to compute the paths and thus the factor loadings, I have shown how various factor models could be tested. The ability of the derived factors to reproduce the correlation matrix is the criterion.

Relevance to confirmatory analysis

In confirmatory analysis, of course, we test only one or two models which have been derived from theory or from previous work. We do not have to compare the huge variety of models that is possible. If, for example, we were to postulate models with factors correlated at 0.1, 0.12, 0.13, right through to 0.99, we would be doing nothing other than rotating the factors. Rather, models should be based on theory or on previous work. For example, in the field of personality it is now claimed (e.g. Digman 1990) that five factors account for most of the variance in personality questionnaires. Furthermore, it is also postulated, in this theory, how certain variables should load on the factors. A five factor model with certain loadings specified would be set up and tested, as has been described.

This, then, is the essence of confirmatory analysis. These path diagrams and the associated path analysis and comparison of the derived correlation matrix with the original correlations illustrate the process of confirmatory analysis. Several points are worthy of further notice.

1 In our worked example, the diagram was just determined so that an exact solution was possible. In cases with latent variables the simultaneous equations have no exact solution so that complex algebraic methods have to be used. This is one of the functions of the computer programs available for confirmatory analysis. However, the principle is no different from the simple case.
2 It was pointed out that all path diagrams could be represented by equivalent structural equations. These, however, do not form the basis of the computing methods of the programs, since these use equivalent matrix algebra methods.
3 In confirmatory analysis some of the unknowns, the path coefficients (or their equivalents in the structural equations), are fixed. These (usually factor loadings but sometimes also correlations between factors) are what the confirmatory analysis seeks to test. Can an adequate (in terms of reproducing the observed correlations) factor analysis be performed constrained by these values?
4 If the resulting residual matrix is small, then the confirmatory analysis can be said to have supported the hypothesis or the model instantiated in the factors. Conversely if the fit is poor the model has to be rejected.

Testing for the goodness of fit

It should be clear from our discussion of confirmatory analysis that the goodness of fit tests are highly important. This is particularly the case because, as shall be seen, some factor analysts are critical of the confirmatory approach because they believe that these tests are not sufficiently discriminating. Hypotheses are both too easily accepted and too easily rejected. The following points can be made.

1 In the iterative solutions of the simultaneous equations goodness of fit tests are used to select the final solution. Thus in the first trial set of values, which is simply to get the process started, the implied correlations are compared with the observed. On the strength of this comparison, the values are modified and a new

comparison is made until the fit is as good as possible or further changes make the fit less good.

2 The best solution having been obtained the goodness of fit of the model can also be evaluated. The different methods of testing goodness of fit are differently suited to these two tasks.

I shall say little about the first use of the goodness of fit tests in solving the simultaneous equations. This is because these are simply part of the algebra of the programs used in confirmatory analysis. However, as should be obvious from the description of the process of iteration, the goodness of fit test has to be done many times. Thus for the first purpose the test should be quick and cheap to compute and ideally it should be useful in showing how the values should be modified to improve the solutions.

In fact there are various complex algebraic methods available for the iterative solution of simultaneous equations of this kind, but their explication is left to specialist texts. LISREL, as might be expected, uses highly efficient methods.

The second use of goodness of fit tests (to test the fit of the model, the simultaneous equations having been solved) is of more importance to the user of confirmatory analysis because most programs will compute all types.

Since the mathematics of these goodness of fit tests is complex and beyond the necessities of the *Easy Guide*, I shall concentrate on the practical issues of their use. Loehlin (1987) contains a clear, introductory discussion of their mathematical basis. There are three goodness of fit tests.

1 The least squares criterion is the simplest to understand. The squared differences of the implied and observed values are squared and added. Where the fit is perfect these are obviously zero. This criterion is quick and cheap to compute where this is important.

2 Generalized least squares is a scaled form of least squares in which the matrix of differences is multiplied by the inverse of the matrix of the observed correlations or covariances. This has the advantage over the first method that the goodness of fit can be subjected to statistical tests.

3 Maximum likelihood methods are also amenable to statistical tests of significance, although their computational procedures are beyond the scope of this book.

The statistical tests used with generalized least squares and maximum likelihood methods   As was mentioned above, the statistical significance of the goodness of fit attained by both these methods can be tested. For this the value of the criterion at the point of best fit is multiplied by $N - 1$ (N being the sample size) and the resulting coefficient can be treated as a χ^2.

Relative efficiency of these goodness of fit tests   As might be expected, a large number of comparisons have been made between the effectiveness of these three tests of fit. The questions asked include whether the same findings would be regarded as confirming the model by all three methods. If they differ, under what conditions does one methods show that the model fits when the others do not and so on. The question of sample size has also been raised.

Loehlin (1987) contains a detailed discussion of these questions but I shall attempt to summarize the rather confused outcomes of these comparisons.

1 Where the original data are normally distributed the maximum likelihood method seems to yield a reliable χ^2. Where the distribution is not normal the generalized least squares method may be preferable.
2 For these statistical test to be reliable, an N of 100 is suggested as minimum, and this is only where simple models with only two factors, say, are proposed. Where the models are more complex Loehlin argues that 500 is a not unreasonable sample size.
3 In some cases there are disagreements. Thus Loehlin cites an instance where the least squares methods agree that one matrix of two matrices resembles a target matrix while the maximum likelihood method selects the other matrix. This is likely to occur when there is not close agreement between the implied and the observed matrix. The larger the sample, however, the less likely are such discrepancies.

The meaning of the goodness of fit tests

Let us ignore, for the moment, the problems of whether the χ^2 test is accurate and consider its meaning.

Suppose that our obtained χ^2 was 12.1. Suppose that with the appropriate degrees of freedom the χ^2 required to reject the null hypothesis at the 0.01 level is 11.34 (these figures are obtained from statistical tables). Our obtained χ^2 is larger than this which means that the null hypothesis must be rejected. The null hypothesis states that the derived correlations and the observed correlations are from the same population and that any differences are due to sampling error. However, the χ^2 being larger than 11.34 means that this has to be rejected. Thus the coefficients are different and it must be concluded that the model does not fit the data.

In brief if χ^2 exceeds the appropriate figure in the statistical tables then the model fails to fit the data. χ^2 is used to show that models do not fit the data.

However, let us now suppose that our obtained χ^2 was only 2.9. This means that the null hypothesis cannot be rejected. This implies that the model cannot be rejected. It does not mean that the model is right; rather it has not been shown that the model is wrong. There are several implications of these arguments.

1 If samples are large χ^2 can easily reach significance, and thus models can be rejected which on examination of the derived and observed correlations or covariances are really quite close.
2 If samples are small, it is possible to accept as fits models which are in fact quite discrepant from the data.
3 The fact that one model fits the data (e.g. a three factor model) does not imply that another model would not also fit. It becomes important, therefore, to test other models. However, the χ^2 test is relatively insensitive and in practice several different models may apparently fit the data.
4 There are problems with the statistical significance to be adopted with the χ^2. At best it should be used as a guide and in all cases the actual discrepancies between implied and observed correlations should be examined. In general, of course, the smaller χ^2 is the better.

Some other statistical tests

In attempt to overcome these problems other statistical tests of the fit of models to data have been calculated for confirmatory analysis. These are described in detail by Loehlin (1987) and I shall not go through them here except to comment on those which may be found in LISREL, which is the usual computer program for confirmatory analysis.

1 *RMR (root mean square residual)*. This is the square root of the mean of the squared discrepancies of the obtained and implied correlations. There is no significance test for this index which varies between 0 and 1 and should be as small as possible (like the simple least squares criterion).

2 *GFI (goodness of fit index)*. This is the ratio of the sum of the squared discrepancies to the observed variances. This ratio takes different scales into account. There is no significance test for this index which again varies between 0 and 1. In this case the closer to 1 the better the fit.

Sufficient has now been said to understand the essence of confirmatory factor analysis. For further information the most useful reference is the one which I have already cited, that of Loehlin (1987). To conclude this chapter I shall discuss some of the problems with confirmatory factor analysis which are sometimes overlooked by enthusiasts for the method. I can do this briefly simply because most of them have been mentioned already in the discussion.

1 The first problem concerns the numbers needed for reliable results, especially if maximum likelihood methods are used which is the approach of LISREL. Nunnally (1978), who is certainly conservative in this respect, argues that to avoid chance effects a ratio of 20:1 for subjects to variables is required. We have already seen that 500 subjects was regarded as not an excessively large sample for studies with relatively few factors. This constraint of sample size may well be a difficulty unless the research has considerable resources of time and money.

2 As has been seen, the statistical tests of whether the hypothesis should be accepted or rejected are not that reliable. When N is large, as it should be for confirmatory analysis, it is easy to reject hypotheses which are really quite well supported. Furthermore, the methods are not good at selecting between competing hypotheses. Since, in addition, there is some doubt as to the appropriate significance of the χ^2, we must conclude that these statistical tests of fit must be treated with great caution.

3 In some cases it is difficult to set a target matrix simply because there is not enough known about the field. This is often the case in psychological studies of personality, for example. Often investigators simply indicate a few high loadings (greater than 0.5) with the rest as zero loadings. Such crude targets are relatively

easy to fit and the results must be interpreted accordingly. Of course, where the attempt is made to target an actual factor analysis, perhaps from another sample, this problem does not arise.

At this point I shall introduce a topic which is strictly not part of confirmatory analysis (as here defined) but which must be mentioned and which fits neatly into this section. There is a method of rotating factors to a target matrix and is known as Procrustes rotation. This was used by Guilford to confirm his model of intelligence which posited 120 factors. By Procrustes rotations Guilford (1967) confirmed many of his factors. However, Horn and Knapp (1973) showed that target matrices could be reached with random data and with data which contained factors antithetical to the targets. Only when matrices are specified with high precision, which is usually not possible, could Procrustes fail. For this reason, I shall not discuss this method further as it cannot be recommended.

4   In the previous chapter it was shown that simple structure was the best account of the field because it was the most parsimonious and because it was generally replicable. In addition it was shown that simple structure solutions did include the most important causal determinants.

   This of course calls into question the meaning of a confirmatory analysis if it is not simple structure. Since most personality theories, for example, are not well supported, the provenance of the target matrix, if theoretically based, has to be carefully scrutinized. In other words there are difficulties in interpreting a clash between a confirmatory and a simple structure factor analysis. This leads on to the last problem.

5   It must never be forgotten that a confirmatory analysis may reject a target matrix. However, if it does not, it means only that the data could fit the target. This does not prove that the hypothetical matrix is correct. It could well be that the data could fit a variety of other targets.

CONCLUSIONS

The conclusions from this discussion are clear cut. Confirmatory analysis is highly useful in testing hypotheses. However, in interpreting the results what it means to say that the data fit the hypotheses must not be forgotten. Similarly the problems of statistical significance and the need for large samples must be remembered as must the nature of the original target matrix.

Finally, it should be realized that confirmatory factor analysis is only one part of LISREL (the measurement model) and that the structural model dealing with relationships between latent variables is highly important for psychological research. The structural modelling branch of path analysis, however, goes beyond the scope of this chapter and book. However, it is a field which, after factor analysis has been mastered, is worthy of pursuit. Confirmatory analysis is a useful introduction to it.

Chapter 7

The interpretation and use of factor analysis: examples from personality testing

In this and the next two chapters I shall take some examples of published factor analyses and subject them to detailed scrutiny. I shall highlight those aspects of the published papers which are essential to the proper use of factor analysis. These are as follows.

1 *The questions which the research was trying to answer.* This is a vital aspect, as should be obvious of any research. Yet all too often, factor analyses are conducted almost for their own sake: to many researchers factor analysis is the Everest of techniques which must be climbed because it is there in the computer package.

   In this and the next two chapters I shall attempt to indicate what problems factor analysis is suited to solve and conversely what it is unable to deal with. Powerful as the technique is there are questions which are more efficiently answered by other methods.

2 *The factor analytic methodology.* Here I shall discuss the technical aspects of the factor analysis, most of which have been explicated in previous chapters. I shall carefully go through the sampling of subjects and variables and the type of factor analysis and rotation to see to what extent the results are likely to be distorted by the methods and whether simple structure has been reached.

   In some instances we shall see how flaws in the methods have infirmed the results and we shall be able to suggest how the study might be improved.

3 *Naming and interpreting the factors.* It is quite possible to carry out technically adequate factor analyses and to fail to interpret the factors correctly. Thus, for example, a factor may be labelled without regard to similar factors which have emerged from other studies. In other cases the fact that a factor is correlated with

other factors may be ignored. Even more importantly I shall examine the reasons for interpreting and naming a factor. This process will be most helpful in seeing how factors are interpreted.

THE SELECTION OF EXAMPLES

I shall choose examples from published research, and in some cases from theses, which illustrate how factor analysis can be used to solve a variety of different problems. Thus at the end of the three chapters of examples I hope that readers will have a good idea of the range of problems which can be tackled by factor analysis. In addition the examples will be such as to illustrate the problems of the methodology.

It might be thought that because the illustrations are taken largely from published papers there would not be severe methodological difficulties. This, unfortunately, is far from the case, as shall be seen. However, even where the techniques are good, I shall explain why the authors chose to use their particular methods. For this reason I have selected projects which I and my colleagues have carried out over many years of psychometric research. I know better than is possible with the work of others why we did what we did. Obviously we have not used all the techniques or exemplified all the applications and to complete the picture the work of other factor analysts is discussed.

It must be stressed that I am discussing our work in a critical fashion because it illustrates the problems of factor analysis. It is not, as will be clear from the discussion, because I believe it to be the finest factor analysis in the world. Would it were.

EXPLORATORY ANALYSIS

Exploratory analysis, as has been made clear, is by far the most common form of factor analysis and most of my examples will be necessarily concerned with this, rather than exploratory or path analysis.

Exploratory analysis can be used for many purposes and in these illustrative chapters I treat the various applications separately.

Demonstrating what a test measures

In psychology and the social sciences variables are measured by tests of many kinds: questionnaires, rating scales or more formal psychological tests. There are huge numbers of these and few of them measure what they claim to measure, as has been fully shown by Kline (1992). This is a serious problem of which many researchers in the social sciences are blissfully unaware. Results from tests which are invalid (do not measure what they claim) are worthless.

EXAMPLE A1: MEASURING THE AUTHORITARIAN PERSONALITY (KLINE AND COOPER 1984b)

Background to the study

In *The Authoritarian Personality* (Adorno *et al.* 1950) a constellation of personality traits was described as characterizing the fascist – obedience to authority and the desire to control both being highly important and both seen as attempts to relieve anxiety. The measures used in that work have been heavily criticized and since that date other tests of authoritarian personality have been developed.

However, factor analytic studies of personality have failed to reveal an authoritarian personality and as a result this is a variable of apparent importance which has become neglected and overlooked in modern work on personality.

Aim of the study

To discover whether different measures of authoritarianism measured the same thing and if this was the case whether this variable was measured by the best factor analytic tests.

Factor analytic design

Factor analysis is ideal to answer these questions. Thus the best factor analytic tests and the best measures of the authoritarian personality should be submitted to a simple structure factor analysis. There are the following possible answers.

1 All the authoritarian scales load on one factor. This demonstrates

that they measure the same variable. The higher the loading the better the test.

2 Some authoritarian scales load one factor, while others load other different factors. This means some of the scales are measuring the same variable.

3 Other scales loading this authoritarian factor, if it emerges, must be inspected to see if they support the validity of the factor as one of authoritarianism.

4 The authoritarian scales simply load on other personality factors. This implies that it is not a useful concept in personality.

5 The scales neither load on one factor nor on any of the other personality factors. This implies that the scales are not correlated and are measuring little but specific variance.

From this it is clear that a factor analysis of the best authoritarian scales together with the other main personality factors is a powerful technique for establishing the validity of the scales.

There is one important point to note about this factor analytic design which is crucial for establishing the validity of a test but which is frequently omitted, especially by users rather than specialists in factor analysis. This is the inclusion of scales in the factor analysis other than the authoritarian measures. Let us suppose that only authoritarian scales had been included in the analysis and let us further suppose that they had all, or at least the majority, loaded on one factor. All this would have shown is that they were measuring the same variable or factor. However, it would not have demonstrated that this variable was the authoritarian personality. For example, if the scales measured anxiety they would all load the same factor. This is why in studies of this sort it is essential that the scales to be investigated are factored with the main relevant factors. Which factors these are will depend, of course, on the type of test.

This type of factor analytic design is called locating the scales in factor space. I shall cite a study of objective tests, later in this chapter, where the inclusion of other scales radically transformed the interpretation of the results.

Sample

A sample of 94 volunteer students (48 males, 46 females) was used.

Tests

There were too many authoritarian tests to include all of them in this study. However, tests were selected against the following criteria.

1 There were to be no common items in the scales, which produce correlations artefactually.
2 Balanced scales were used (those with equal numbers of 'yes' and 'no' keyed responses). This eliminates the response set of acquiescence, agreeing with items regardless of content.
3 Other similar syndromes, such as dogmatism, conservatism and anal character were covered.
4 The criticism that authoritarian scales were only right wing was taken into account.

On these criteria five scales were selected.

1 Ai3Q: a measure of anal character.
2 The Wilson–Patterson conservatism scale.
3 The Ray balanced dogmatism scale.
4 Kohn's balanced F scale.
5 Machiavellian scales: these were included because it was felt that these might measure little more than authoritarianism.

To locate these tests in personality factor space two well-established sets of personality factors were used – those of Eysenck and Cattell.

6 Eysenck's EPQ test measuring the biggest second–order factors (see Chapter 5) – neuroticism (or anxiety), extraversion and psychoticism.
7 Cattell's 16PF test which measures 16 primary personality factors including intelligence.

Factor analytic method

Principal components; Scree test (selecting five factors); principal factors; oblique Direct Oblimin rotation.

Comments on method

Before the results of this study can be interpreted it is necessary to discuss the method. As was pointed out in Chapter 5, it has been shown that a Direct Oblimin rotation of the factors selected by the Scree test is about the most efficient way of reaching simple structure. This aspect of the study, therefore, would appear perfectly satisfactory.

However, the sampling is less satisfactory. As was fully discussed, the larger the sample size the more reliable the factor analysis. The sample size in this study (94) is far less than would be desired. With such a sample the results would have to fit previous work before they could be acceptable.

Even less satisfactory is the fact that the subjects are all students. This limits the variance, although in a study of this type this is likely to make it less easy than with a more heterogeneous sample to find clear factors. It would certainly have been better to have had a larger sample and one reflecting more closely a general population.

Since we were testing the hypothesis that there is one authoritarian factor and that there are also factors of anxiety and extraversion, a confirmatory analysis might be thought a superior strategy. However, the small numbers in the sample and the consequent problems with the χ^2 test make this a dubious option.

Results

The results are set out in Table 7.1 which shows the Direct Oblimin rotated factor analysis and the correlations between factors.

Interpretation of factors

This factor analysis has clarified what the tests measure.

Factor 1

Factor 1 loads on all the authoritarian scales. This is a clear authoritarian factor and Kohn's F scale would appear to be the best measure.

Examination of the other scales loading this factor is instructive. Thus Cattell's G scale, conscientiousness or superego, and Q3 scale, self-sentiment and control, load this factor. This makes good psychological sense. Similarly the negative loading on Eysenck's P scale, which involves risk taking and breaking conventions, fits the

Table 7.1 Direct Oblimin rotated factor structure matrix

Variables	Factor				
	1	2	3	4	5
Ai3	0.60	−0.11	0.10	−0.04	−0.08
Wilson–Patterson military	0.40	0.15	−0.18	0.04	0.08
Wilson–Patterson anti-hedonism	0.54	−0.01	0.60	−0.16	−0.15
Wilson–Patterson ethnocentrism	0.40	0.11	0.22	−0.14	0.37
Wilson–Patterson religion	0.53	−0.06	0.52	0.02	−0.09
Balanced dogmatism	0.23	−0.27	0.52	−0.14	0.31
Machiavellian tactics	0.16	0.01	−0.75	−0.05	0.00
Machiavellian views	0.02	−0.15	−0.49	−0.22	0.15
Machiavellian morality	−0.23	−0.08	−0.73	0.02	0.08
Kohn's F scale	0.84	0.11	−0.01	0.18	−0.20
EPQ E extraversion	−0.07	0.13	−0.05	0.87	0.12
EPQ N neuroticism	−0.10	−0.87	0.04	−0.37	−0.13
EPQ P psychoticism	−0.53	−0.03	−0.34	0.16	0.27
EPQ L Lie scale	0.10	0.06	0.33	−0.28	0.14
16PF A sociality	0.15	−0.22	0.00	0.27	0.00
16PF B intelligence	−0.08	0.17	0.07	−0.18	0.24
16PF C ego-strength	−0.00	0.61	0.18	0.12	0.10
16PF E dominance	−0.11	0.08	−0.11	0.48	0.70
16PF F cheerfulness	−0.13	0.03	−0.16	0.73	0.12
16PF G conscientious	0.67	0.21	0.20	−0.07	−0.03
16PF H adventurous	−0.05	0.30	0.12	0.69	0.37
16PF I tough minded	−0.09	−0.43	0.38	0.01	−0.36
16PF L suspiciousness	−0.14	−0.30	−0.18	0.18	0.47
16PF M unconventionality	−0.32	0.09	−0.03	0.09	0.09
16PF N shrewdness	0.23	−0.14	0.08	−0.23	−0.46
16PF O guilt feelings	−0.08	−0.77	0.07	0.07	−0.23
16PF Q1 radicalism	−0.31	0.03	−0.36	0.12	0.45
16PF Q2 independence	−0.00	0.12	−0.10	−0.27	0.00
16PF Q3 self-sentiment	0.55	0.33	0.11	−0.21	−0.15
16PF Q4 tension	−0.17	−0.76	0.05	0.05	0.07
Percentage of total variance accounted for	14.2	12.0	11.6	10.0	7.8

Factor intercorrelations

Factor 1					
Factor 2	0.044				
Factor 3	0.095	−0.113			
Factor 4	−0.107	−0.099	−0.122		
Factor 5	0.027	0.085	0.055	0.963	

Notes: Hyperplane count, 41%; hyperplane width, ±0.1; δ, −0.6.

factor. There can be little doubt that this factor 1 is clear evidence of an authoritarian factor of control.

Finally it should be noted that Eysenck's L scale, measuring social desirability, and Cattell's B scale, intelligence, do not load the authoritarian factor. This destroys the objection to the authoritarian scales that they are influenced by intelligence and by the response set of social desirability.

I shall not discuss the other factors in this analysis in any detail since they are not so pertinent to the aims of this study, which were to investigate the status of the authoritarian personality and the quality of the scales purporting to measure it. However, their interpretation is useful for understanding factor analysis.

Factor 2

This is clearly the anxiety factor with its large loading on Eysenck's N scale and Cattell's C scale, ego strength. Notice that the sign of the factor loadings is relative. Thus the fact that the N loading is negative means that the factor was scored for stability rather than anxiety – the opposite end of the scale. However, the meaning is identical. Thus Cattell's ego strength has a positive loading. It would be possible to reverse the signs in this factor (or any factor) without in any way changing its interpretation. This I hope clarifies the nature of reflecting the residual matrix, where the signs were changed, in the calculation of principal components analysis, described in Chapter 3.

Factor 3

This loads mainly the Machiavellian scales but also has loadings on some of the authoritarian scales, although these are not as large as on factor 1. There are two points of interest here from the viewpoint of interpreting factors. First, although factors 1 and 3 are not correlated they do share some common variance on some of the authoritarian scales. Actually the fact that some of the authoritarian scales load both factors is a useful criterion for selecting between them. It is better if scales are factor pure since any given score must then have an identical meaning. This is not true if a test measures two factors for obvious reasons. Thus the factor pure scales would be preferred – in this instance the Kohn and Ai3 scales.

Factor 4

By looking at the largest loadings it is clear that this factor is extraversion. It loads on Eysenck's E and on the Cattell's extraversion scales. Factor 5 is not easy to name and I shall not discuss it further here.

A further point should be noted about this factor analysis. The main personality factors of extraversion and neuroticism or anxiety emerged with great clarity. This supports the adequacy of the factor analysis – since these are marker factors in the field of personality – and adds some weight to the emergence of the authoritarian factor. It also goes some way to overcoming the technical defects of the analysis which were discussed earlier in this section.

From this scrutiny of this factor analysis I hope that a number of points about interpreting factors become clear.

1 The largest loadings give the clue to the identification of the factors.
2 A check needs to be made that the zero or low loadings confirm the identification.
3 The signs of the loadings are only relatively and not absolutely important.
4 The factor purity of scales can be judged by examining the relevant rows of the factor matrix. Tests should load only one factor.

Conclusions

This study has been able to answer the questions it was designed to investigate. It demonstrates that with the proper selection of variables and with careful rotational procedures the nature of test variables can be explicated. It is difficult to argue, given this study, that authoritarian personality is not a useful personality variable and that it is simply measured in the work of Cattell and Eysenck, although the P scale and Cattell's G scale are not far away from this factor.

EXAMPLE A2: INVESTIGATING THE TYPE A BEHAVIOUR PATTERN (MAY AND KLINE 1987)

Background to the study

The type A behaviour pattern, characterized by impatience, speed, hard-driving, competitiveness and emotional repression, has been associated with heart disease. Thus if it were a genuine syndrome of personality traits it might be important in preventative medicine and of considerable theoretical interest.

Type A is not of itself a factor but is claimed to be a mixture of neuroticism and extraversion, the neurotic extravert being essentially the type A personality. However, as May and Kline (1987) demonstrated, empirical studies usually fail to show extraversion in fact correlating to any extent with measures of type A.

Aim of the study

The aim of this study was to clarify the relation of type A personality to extraversion, neuroticism and obsessionality, the latter being chosen because it is one of the regularly appearing personality factors and because its central characteristic – control – is an aspect of the type A personality.

Sample

A sample of 135 male soldiers, aged 18–25 was used.

Tests

1 Thirty-one item subset of the Jenkins Activity Survey (JAS), a well-known measure of type A personality.
2 The EPQ test, measuring the largest personality factors: extraversion, neuroticism (anxiety) and psychoticism.
3 The Ai3Q test, a measure of obsessional personality traits. This test loaded highly on the authoritarian factor of our previous example.

It should be noted that a shortened version of the JAS had to be used because some of the items in the original scale were unsuited to military personnel. However, the factor analysis to be carried out in this study will reveal whether this short scale was invalid.

Factor analysis

The correlations between the items of the JAS were subjected to a principal components analysis. The Scree test selected four factors and both four and three factors (found by some other investigators) were rotated to oblique simple structure by Direct Oblimin. Factor scores were computed and these were correlated with the scores from the EPQ and Ai3Q tests.

Results

Table 7.2 The four factor solution of the shortened type A scale

Item	Correlation	Text of 'type A' answer (précis)
Factor 1: Impatience		
3	0.68	Feel like hurrying slow talkers
17	0.51	Hurry to get places, even if plenty of time
13	0.48	Irritated if interrupted during important task
23	0.44	Frequently make written lists to remember tasks
1	0.43	Do two things at once whenever practical
4	0.39	Put words into other person's mouth to speed them up
18	0.39	I get things done while waiting if someone else late
24	0.35	Angered if person ahead in queue is slow
19	0.33	Others agree that I do most things in a hurry
27	0.33	Others agree that I get irritated easily
29	0.30	Refuse to queue, find ways to avoid such delays
22	0.30	I regularly do risky things for excitement
Factor 2: Hard-driving/competitive		
10	0.68	Nowadays I am definitely hard-driving and competitive
11	0.64	Others would rate me as hard-driving and competitive
20	0.57	Others would not say I have less energy than most
21	0.50	Others would agree I enjoy contests and try to win
15	0.39	If I arrange to meet at a definite time I am never late
22	0.39	I regularly do risky things for excitement
27	−0.37	Others agree that I get irritated easily
12	0.36	Others would rate me as too active – I should slow down
28	0.35	Top executives succeed through hard work
2	0.31	I take over job if beginner doing it slower than I would
Factor 3: Speed		
6	0.77	Others tell me I eat too fast
5	0.74	When I eat I'm usually the first to finish
19	0.59	Others agree that I do most things in a hurry
18	0.40	I get things done while waiting if someone else is late
8	0.36	It really stirs me up if my team loses
12	0.36	Others would rate me as too active – I should slow down

| 7 | 0.33 | In team games I'm only satisfied if better than others |

Factor 4: Unrepressed

26	0.64	Nowadays my temper is fiery and hard to control
27	0.57	Others agree that I get irritated easily
9	0.56	I enjoy competition because it is stimulating
25	0.52	When younger my temper was fiery and hard to control
21	0.47	Others would agree that I enjoy contests and try to win
11	0.37	Others would rate me as hard-driving and competitive
8	0.36	It really stirs me up if my team loses
12	0.34	Others would rate me as too active – I should slow down
10	0.33	Nowadays I am definitely hard-driving and competitive
7	0.30	In team games I'm only satisfied if better than others

No correlations > 0.3 with any factors

14		If interruptions have angered me I say so firmly
16		In last ten years I've not been late for scheduled events
30		I find it very difficult to relax after hard day
31		When I get tired on the job I keep pushing

Table 7.3 sets out the correlations between the factor scores and the personality tests.

Table 7.3 Correlations between factor scores and psychometric variables

Factor	Description	E	N	P	Ai3
1	Impatience	−0.07	0.20*	0.07	0.19*
2	Hard-driving/Competitive	0.33**	−0.37**	−0.14	0.04
3	Speed	−0.12	0.24*	0.13	0.19*
4	Unrepressed	0.29**	0.13	0.11	0.25*
	Total 'type A' score	0.14	0.12	0.02	0.37*
		←	$n = 122$	→	$n = 124$

Notes: *, $p < 0.05$; **, $p < 0.001$.

Comments

The fact that we have used the same tests in these two examples is not coincidental. The EPQ test, and to a lesser extent the Ai3Q test, are good markers for the factors which they measure. They are useful, therefore, in locating personality factors in space.

Similarly the fact that we used Direct Oblimin in both studies does not mean that this is the only rotational method which could be used. It simply reflects the fact that this program has been shown to be efficient at attaining simple structure.

There are several points which should be noted about the use of factor analysis in this study.

1   As was made clear in our chapter on rotation the various tests for the numbers of factors to extract are only guidelines. Thus the fact that the Scree test indicated four factors does not preclude the rotation of three. It should be noted that the criterion of eigenvalues greater than 1 indicated ten factors, which with only 31 items is clearly far too many.
2   We might have used maximum likelihood analysis to select the number of factors on a statistical basis and despite the efficiency of the Scree test this might have been preferable.
3   We ran principal components rather than factors. Ideally principal factors is the better procedure, for reasons which have been given (see Chapter 4), although in practice there is little difference.

All these are minor points. However, there is a more important issue to be considered about the methods used in this study.

4   Notice that we did not simply factor all the items in all the tests. This was because we had insufficient subjects in the study. However, correlations between the factor scores of the JAS items and the personality scales answer all the questions which this study posed.
5   There is a further important point to notice about this factor analytic design. By correlating the item factors with other scales we ensure that the item factors of the JAS are not simply bloated specifics.

Bloated specifics, a term used by Cattell (e.g. 1978), look like factors but are really only specific variance. They can be produced very easily by writing items which are essentially paraphrases of each other. These not surprisingly correlate highly and thus form a factor. Specific factors can only be discriminated from common factors by the fact that they correlate with no other factors or external criteria. Thus the device of correlating the JAS item factors with other different scales demonstrates that the factors are not bloated specifics and provides answers to the original questions of this experiment – namely what is the relationship of the type A personality to the major variables recognized by factor analysis.

Interpretation of the factors

The item factors in Table 7.2 were interpreted from the content of the items which loaded on them. The content of the highest loading items is the key to the identification of the factors, although it should be noted that this is little more than face validity. Factor 1 was labelled impatience since most of the items were concerned with hurrying and hating waiting. Again it should be noted that a set of such items could easily be a bloated specific. Factor 2 as the first two items indicate was labelled hard driving or competitive. Factor 3 was speed. Notice that item 18 loaded on both factor 1 and this factor. This is hardly surprising. Factor 4 was identified as uncontrolled. All these factors had intercorrelations of less than 0.11.

Discussion

These results were similar to those of other workers although in this study speed and impatience were separate factors which is not always the case. In the three factor solution the speed factor disappeared with some of its items going to factor 1 and the others to factor 4.

Even in this shortened form there is a clear factor structure to the JAS. Since these factors are not highly correlated it makes little sense to score the JAS as one scale since it is obvious that any given score will not be equivalent (being composed of four variables or factors) except by chance.

Correlations with the other tests

Examination of Table 7.3 is revealing. Thus with extraversion hard driving and unrepressed correlate significantly while the other factors do not and are actually negative.

With the N factor the case is even more striking, since two of the factors are positively correlated while one is negatively related.

Both these examples show the error of measuring the type A personality with a single test, since it is a syndrome which is not factorially homogeneous, although it should be noted that there is a correlation between the total score on type A and obsessional character.

Conclusions

This factor analysis has shown that although type A may form a syndrome or pattern of personality traits they are not sufficiently homogeneous to be measured in a single scale. The items of the JAS fall into several factors (even though a few items load more than one factor). These different factor have quite different correlations with the best established dimensions of personality, thus making nonsense of correlations with the JAS total score.

This is a clear instance of how factor analysis can reveal the nature of personality variables and account for the confusion of results which is so often found.

EXAMPLE A3: INVESTIGATING FIVE NEW PERSONALITY SCALES (KLINE *ET AL.* 1987)

Background to the study

Auld has developed a picture preference test (PPT) which involves subjects selecting which pictures they liked from 266 pictures presented in pairs. The rationale was that choice was determined by approach avoidance tendencies and that by having many cards apparently tapping the same theme a scale may be developed. In this study six scales with reasonably good reliabilities were used. However, despite the names (based on the content of the pictures selected) there was no independent evidence as to the validity of these scales.

Aim of the study

To investigate what these six PPT scales measured.

Factor analytic design

As with the other examples the aim was to locate these scales in factor space. To do this the Auld scales were factored with the main marker factors in the fields of personality and ability. Notice that ability factors were also included because it could have been the case that preference for these tests depended on abilities as well as personality.

Subjects

A sample of 182 students, mean age 20 years, of which there were 83 men and 99 women, was used.

Tests

1 Five scales from the Auld test: maladjustment; impulse control; avoidance of sexual intimacy; antisocial impulses; primary-process thinking; introversion.
2 The comprehensive ability battery (CAB). This measures the main ability factors: verbal ability; numerical ability; spatial ability; speed of closure; perceptual speed; inductive reasoning; flexibility of closure; rote memory; mechanical knowledge; memory span; meaningful memory; spelling ability; aesthetic judgement; spontaneous flexibility; ideational fluency; word fluency; originality.
3 Personality factors. As might be expected we used the marker factors of the previous studies: EPQ, measuring extraversion, neuroticism and psychoticism; Cattell 16PF test, measuring 16 primary personality factors; and the authoritarian and Machiavellian scales which have been described in example A1.

Factor analysis

Our usual procedure for rotation to simple structure was followed: principal components; the Scree test for the number of factors; principal factors; Direct Oblimin oblique rotation.

Comments on method

This is the standard method which we have used in all these examples for exploratory analysis. As is argued in Chapter 5 this set of procedures generally reaches simple structure (see Cattell 1978, or Carroll 1983). If I were carrying out this study today, with improved programs and computing facilities, I would also use a maximum likelihood factor analysis to investigate the accuracy of the Scree test.

Results

The factor pattern matrix is set out in Table 7.4.

Comments

I shall not interpret all the factors in this table but only those relevant to our question – what do the Auld PPT scales measure? However, two further points need to be discussed before interpretation can begin. First, it must be noted that the pattern matrix rather than the structure matrix has been used. The loadings, therefore, are the weights to be used for predicting the variables rather than the correlations of the structure matrix. The pattern matrix differs from the structure matrix in that the weights take into account the fact that the factors are correlated. In the orthogonal case weights and correlations are identical (see Chapters 4 and 5). In this study, however, the correlations between the orthogonal factors were so low that the pattern and structure matrix were virtually identical. I would still prefer to see the structure matrix for reasons which have been discussed. However, we may interpret this pattern matrix as if the loadings were correlations.

There are two omissions from this table. First, the ability variables from the CAB have not been included. This is because none of them loaded the PPT factors and they are therefore irrelevant. Second, some factors have been left out of the table. These loaded only on ability scales.

Before attempting to interpret the PPT factors, it is first necessary to check whether the factor analysis is satisfactory and to see whether the marker factors have emerged as expected. If they have not it suggests that, for some reason, simple structure has not been obtained. This is particularly important because the subject to variable ratio is not as high as some factorists would like, although it is certainly sufficient to produce a reliable analysis.

Have the marker factors emerged? Fortunately the answer to this question is positive. Thus factor 6 is clearly the extraversion factor, loading on Cattell's E and H scales, extraversion primaries and Eysenck's E scale. Notice here that the negative signs can be ignored.

Factor 1 is equally certainly neuroticism or anxiety, loading on Eysenck's N and Cattell's O scale, guilt proneness, the main anxiety primary factor. Factor 2 is without doubt the authoritarian

Table 7.4 Factor pattern matrix for PPT scales and other variables

Variables	1	2	3	4	6	8	9	10	12
					Factors				
Maladjustment	−0.05	0.08	0.74	−0.09	−0.05	0.07	−0.05	0.07	−0.04
Impulse control	0.01	0.11	−0.30	0.16	0.07	0.53	0.08	−0.11	0.01
Avoidance of sexual intimacy	−0.13	−0.02	−0.17	−0.17	0.06	−0.07	0.09	0.31	−0.15
Antisocial impulses	0.09	0.05	0.86	0.04	−0.04	−0.10	−0.07	−0.13	0.10
Primary process	−0.04	−0.05	0.79	−0.03	0.05	−0.19	0.07	0.10	0.08
PPT introversion	0.03	−0.04	−0.10	−0.05	−0.06	0.02	0.05	0.01	−0.27
Ai3	−0.22	0.52	−0.13	−0.08	−0.05	0.03	−0.04	0.11	0.12
Militarism	0.02	0.78	0.15	−0.02	0.01	0.09	−0.13	−0.07	0.02
Antihedonism	0.05	0.34	−0.10	−0.56	0.08	0.01	0.16	0.18	−0.07
Ethnocentrism	0.06	0.54	0.09	−0.04	−0.01	−0.70	−0.08	0.07	0.14
Religiosity	0.02	0.41	0.13	−0.64	0.12	−0.05	0.10	0.05	−0.06
Balanced dogmatism	−0.19	0.12	0.16	−0.55	−0.09	0.21	0.08	−0.04	0.11
Machiavellian tactics	0.01	0.35	0.15	0.56	0.01	0.22	0.17	0.03	−0.03
Machiavellian views	−0.07	0.22	0.34	0.33	0.01	0.27	0.14	0.17	0.05
Machiavellian morality	−0.18	0.05	0.11	0.70	−0.02	−0.03	0.05	0.04	0.06
Authoritarianism	0.02	0.80	0.02	−0.07	0.11	0.00	0.13	−0.07	−0.07
EPQ Extraversion	0.19	0.29	0.06	0.03	−0.41	−0.36	0.16	−0.27	−0.30
EPQ Neuroticism	−0.86	−0.05	−0.02	0.05	−0.01	−0.11	0.12	−0.02	0.14
EPQ Psychoticism	−0.03	−0.30	0.29	0.23	−0.19	0.22	−0.01	0.03	−0.13
EPQ Lie scale	0.16	−0.02	0.00	−0.21	0.07	0.05	0.16	0.26	0.30
16PF A	0.05	0.14	−0.06	0.02	0.00	0.01	0.29	−0.49	0.06
16PF C	0.74	−0.03	−0.05	−0.02	−0.09	−0.15	0.09	0.02	0.00
16PF E	−0.07	−0.07	−0.10	0.05	−0.91	0.10	−0.02	0.05	−0.04
16PF F	0.11	0.19	0.14	0.15	−0.33	−0.38	0.30	−0.37	−0.19
16PF G	0.07	0.46	−0.29	−0.17	−0.08	0.04	−0.05	−0.09	0.40
16PF H	0.47	0.16	0.07	−0.07	−0.53	−0.15	0.17	−0.12	−0.18
16PF I	−0.08	−0.24	0.00	−0.17	0.16	−0.35	0.45	−0.04	0.11
16PF L	−0.42	0.13	0.25	−0.01	−0.38	0.11	−0.15	−0.09	0.01
16PF M	0.32	−0.25	0.21	0.04	0.06	−0.06	0.04	−0.04	0.02
16PF N	−0.06	0.08	−0.13	0.02	0.51	0.08	0.11	0.01	0.03
16PF O	−0.76	0.00	0.00	0.01	0.09	−0.14	0.08	0.02	−0.05
16PF Q1	0.07	−0.21	0.16	0.35	−0.37	0.09	0.09	0.15	0.16
16PF Q2	0.07	0.09	0.10	0.15	0.02	−0.01	0.03	0.60	0.04
16PF Q3	0.31	0.36	−0.20	0.05	0.21	0.01	−0.05	−0.01	0.36
16PF Q4	−0.86	−0.07	−0.06	0.02	−0.10	−0.13	−0.04	−0.06	−0.03

factor which was found in the first example.

Factors 1, 2 and 6 indicate unequivocally that this factor analysis has identified the main marker factors in the field of personality. Thus we can have confidence in the other factors emerging from it.

Having identified these three factors we are now in a position to answer some important questions concerning the nature of the PPT scales.

1 Do the PPT scales simply measure the main personality factors – extraversion, anxiety and authoritarian or obsessional personality? If any of the PPT scales load on these factors the answer is positive. The answer is clear – none of the PPT scales measure the main personality factors. This certainly means that they are not redundant.
2 Do the PPT scales measure the main ability factors? The answer again is no. Although we do not show the ability factors none of them had loadings on the PPT scales.
3 What do the PPT scales measure? Each scale will now be discussed individually.

PPT introversion

This scale is certainly not valid. It fails to load the marker extraversion factor and it has no loadings on any of the other factors, except possibly 12. This is probably the social desirability scale. However, with its low loading the PPT introversion scale could not be used even for this purpose. It can be concluded that this scale should be abandoned.

PPT avoidance of sexual intimacy

This scale loads only factor 10. From the loadings on the other scales – -0.27 for extraversion, -0.49 for Cattell's A scale (coldness), -0.37 for the F scale (gloomy) and 0.60 for the Q2 scale (group dependent) – this was a clear sociability factor. Thus the loading on the avoidance of sexual intimacy factor makes sense and this factor supports the validity of this PPT scale.

PPT impulse control

This scale loads factor 3, which is the PPT factor and which will be discussed below, and more highly factor 8. However, this is not helpful since this factor is difficult to identify from the other high loadings.

Nevertheless the factor analysis is not useless in the validation of the PPT impulse control. Thus, if valid it should load on the obsessional and authoritarian factor, a factor virtually springing from impulse control and repression. That it does not load on this factor means that it cannot be valid.

It can be concluded that whatever the variance in this scale may be it is not impulse control.

PPT maladjustment, antisocial impulses and primary processes

It will be noticed that these three scales load highly on the third factor, as does impulse control to a lesser extent. From this it could be argued that this is a specific PPT factor arising from the unique format of the test which requires subjects to select one from a pair of pictures many times. However, attractive as this identification might appear it is not satisfactory. This is because if this were the correct identification we would expect all the PPT scales to load this factor, which is not the case, and all the loadings to be highly similar, which again is not true.

The loadings on factor 3 of maladjustment, antisocial impulses and primary processes are such that it is clear that essentially they are measuring the same variable, and this is supported by their intercorrelations which are all around 0.6. If the reliabilities of these scales are taken into account this again suggests that they are not essentially different.

Given that these scales load this factor its identification and thus the meaning of these scales must depend on the loading of the marker tests. Although these loadings are low they are consistent. Thus this factor is loaded on the P scale, psychoticism or tough-mindedness, Machiavellian views and negatively on Cattell's G scale, conscientiousness.

These loadings all suggest that this is a factor of a somewhat antisocial kind and supports the validity of the PPT scales as measuring a variable of maladjustment perhaps not dissimilar to Eysenck's P scale.

This interpretation is supported by the structure matrix loadings which, as has been argued, are easier to interpret, being correlations rather than weights. Thus the structure loadings give greater clarity to the factor. P loads 0.5, G −0.43 and Machiavellian views 0.43. Machiavellian morality and tactics also load the structure factor (0.32 and 0.30 respectively) and three other Cattell factors have salient loadings – Q3 (control) with −0.38, L (suspiciousness) with 0.42 and Q1 (independence) with 0.37.

Conclusions

This factor analysis has demonstrated again how it can clarify the nature of test variables. It has shown that the PPT introversion scale does not measure introversion. It demonstrates similarly that impulse control is not valid. However, it also shows that the avoidance of sexual intimacy scale loads up as is expected and thus supports its validity. Finally, it demonstrates that three PPT scales are essentially identical and are measuring a variable of antisocial personality akin to Eysenck's P scale.

Two other points should be noted about this factor analysis. First using marker variables not only aids the identification of the resulting factors but also works as a check on the adequacy of the factor analysis. Second, it was comparing the factor pattern and structure matrix in studies such as this that caused me to prefer to interpret the structure matrix. It is usually clearer and simpler to understand.

EXAMPLE A4

The last study which I shall discuss in this chapter is an investigation of the validity of the objective–analytic test battery (OATB) (Kline and Cooper 1984a). Since its design is similar to that of our previous examples this aspect of the research can be dealt with more briefly.

Background to the study

Objective personality tests are tests so designed that their purpose cannot be guessed by subjects taking the test. There are many such tests but few of them have ever been validated. This is particularly disappointing since the fact that they are difficult to fake makes them valuable in applied psychology. One such set of tests is the OATB. Since its validity is unknown we decided that it should be examined.

Aim of the study

To discover by location in factor space what the scales in the OATB measured.

Factor analytic design

As with the other examples the OATB was factored with the main marker variables in the field of ability and personality. This would show whether the OATB scales were measuring separate factors and if so how they were related to the markers or whether they overlapped questionnaire measures of personality.

Subjects

A sample of 154 students of whom 75 were males was used.

Test administration

As will be seen a considerable test battery was used to bound the factor space. As a result the testing time was 12 hours. Each subject had four 3-hour sessions.

Comments

The relatively small sample size is accounted for by the difficulty of obtaining subjects prepared to undergo so extensive a testing session. Their only reward was feedback on the results relative to vocational guidance. This study exemplifies the difficulties of obtaining large samples.

Tests

1 *Personality questionnaires*. All the marker scales used in the previous studies were incorporated into this research – the EPQ, the 16PF, measures of obsessionality and authoritarianism and the Machiavellian scales.
2 *Ability scales*. Here the CAB was given. This was selected because it measures all the main ability factors.
3 *The OATB (Cattell and Schuerger 1978)*. This consists of 76 subtests yielding 10 personality factors: assertion; exactness; evasiveness; exuberance; neuroticism; anxiety to achieve; realism–psychoticism; self-assurance; exvia (extraversion); pessimism.

Factor analysis

Two analyses were conducted: one with the scales of the OATB and a second with the factors which had emerged from the OATB in an earlier study. I shall discuss the findings from these separately, but the factor analytic methodology was identical: principal components; selection of factors to rotate using Scree test, Velicer's method (1976) and the criterion of eigenvalues greater than 1; principal factor analysis; Direct Oblimin rotation.

Comments on the method

As was mentioned above, this analysis is the standard design which I use for locating new tests in factor space bounded by marker factors. The technical methods are those which have been shown to attain simple structure. However, in this instance there were problems. The critical issue of the numbers of factors to rotate (see Chapter 4) was not dealt with very well. Thus the Scree test indicated two possibilities, 12 or 9 factors. Another efficient test, Velicer's MAP, was used as a check and this indicated six or nine factors; while the criterion of eigenvalues greater than 1 yielded 16.

Here it would have been sensible to use a maximum likelihood factor analysis to obtain the number of factors to rotate on a statistical basis.

Results: study 1

In fact nine factors were rotated to simple structure. I shall not set out the factor analysis in this case. It is sufficient to note that the four pervasive questionnaire factors of extraversion, anxiety or neuroticism, psychoticism and obsessional or authoritarian factors all emerged, thus demonstrating that despite the problems of rotating the correct number of factors, the results were in accord with previous studies.

As regards the OATB this factor analysis was not encouraging. It could not measure either anxiety or extraversion and many of the factors loaded on ability factors, some being mixtures of personality and ability, others being amalgams of ability factors.

It had to be concluded that the OATB, at least in Great Britain, was not a valid personality test.

Results: study 2

In previous work with the OATB on its own we had found that there were ten factors in the test, although these did not correspond with the ten scales scored by Cattell. In this second study these ten OATB factors were used in place of the scales.

As before there were difficulties over rotating the correct number of factors and finally 13 factors were selected. These factors were more easy to interpret than those in study 1 but again the OATB factors were not factor pure, i.e. they loaded more than one factor. Furthermore they tended again to be amalgams of ability and personality factors.

Thus this factor analysis again was able to explicate the variance in the OATB. It was clear that despite their names the OATB anxiety and extraversion scales were not measuring what the questionnaire variables were measuring and were not valid. Furthermore what factors there were turned out to be confounded by ability. The OATB, at least in Great Britain, on the evidence of these results is not a satisfactory test. The value of including ability factors (although the OATB is a personality test) is self-evident. Had they not been included the test might have appeared to be measuring some unknown personality factors.

GENERAL CONCLUSIONS FROM ALL EXAMPLES

I have described four studies in which my colleagues and I factored a variety of tests to locate them in factor space and thus establish what they were measuring, the nature of their variance. We used a set of marker tests for ability and personality because, at that time, these were the best established personality factors and ability factors. Now I might include different tests as marker factors but the principle would be the same – to locate the test under investigation in factor space.

It is to be noted that this technique is able to show what a test does not measure as well as what it measures, which in the case of the OATB is important since this claimed to be an objective test of extraversion and anxiety.

By using a standard set of marker factors there is the advantage that as studies accumulate a map of the whole field of personality can be drawn and different studies are sensibly comparable.

Finally a word must be said about the technical aspects of the factor analyses used in these investigations. At the time they were conducted these seemed to be the most efficient methods of obtaining simple structure. As was clear, at least from the final example, the vital issue of the number of factors to rotate was not well settled. As I argued in Chapter 5 methods such as the Scree test or the Velicer MAP test are simply convenient algorithms. Where they do not agree, it is best to try several different solutions.

The maximum likelihood approach which has a statistical basis, as was described in Chapter 4, is the favoured technique for selecting the correct number of factors (although problems with this have been noted), but it must be pointed out that in large matrices the difference between maximum likelihood solutions and principal factors is small. Certainly where the Scree test is unclear or where simple structure has not been obtained by the criterion of the hyperplane count, maximum likelihood factor analysis should be computed.

Finally I hope that one function of factor analysis, the clarification of what tests are measuring, has now been exemplified and demonstrated in this chapter. There is no doubt that location in factor space is an important aspect of test validation.

Chapter 8

Factor analysis in test construction

In this chapter I shall discuss the use of factor analysis in the construction of tests, which is another of its major uses in the fields of psychology and education especially. Actually, as shall be seen, understanding the use of factor analysis in test construction is of value to any test user in the social sciences since factor analytic tests are superior to those constructed by other methods.

RATIONALE OF FACTOR ANALYSIS IN TEST CONSTRUCTION

In Chapter 3 it was shown how variance was composed of three components: common factor variance, specific factor variance and error variance. The last two are referred to as the unique variance. Ideally the common factor variance of any variable should be as large as possible and unitary (accounted for by one factor). Thus scores on tests which load more than factor are difficult to interpret since the relative contributions of these factors is unknown.

It follows from this factor analytic model of test variance that factor analysis is the ideal method of test construction. Thus by administering items and subjecting their intercorrelations to factor analysis it is possible to select items which load on only one factor. This ensures that the test is unifactorial.

In this book I do not want to go into the details of factor analytic test construction which I have fully covered in *The Handbook of Psychological Testing* (Kline 1992). Suffice it to say here that there are various technical problems which have led test constructors to use other methods. The most important of these must be briefly mentioned in order that the examples of factor analytic test construction which I shall discuss later in this chapter can be fully understood. In addition I shall mention briefly the alternative methods which are used.

PROBLEMS IN FACTOR ANALYTIC TEST CONSTRUCTION

1 Most items have yes/no responses or perhaps five point rating scales. In ability tests where there is a right and wrong answer the responses are inevitably dichotomized. This means that for each item there is relatively little variability.

2 With dichotomous variables the correlation coefficient has to be chosen with great care. Thus, for example, the tetrachoric correlation has a large standard error. This is fatal for factor analysis unless huge samples are used. In any case strictly this coefficient should not be factored.

   Usually the ϕ coefficient is used. Its value, however, is affected by the item split – the proportion obtaining the correct answer – and this clearly affects the factor analysis.

   Even with five and seven point scales the variability is limited such that Pearson correlations (see Chapter 2) are far from ideal coefficients.

3 Factors derived from item correlations, partly as a result of this problem of the correlation coefficient, tend to account for rather small proportions of variance in the matrix.

4 Test reliability (variance other than error variance) increases with test length. Now an item may be thought of as a one item test. This makes it obvious that items are each extremely unreliable. This adds to the error in the intercorrelations between them and thus lowers the variance accounted for by factors.

5 As was demonstrated in Chapter 3, there is a general factor in principal component and principal factor analysis which is an artefact of the algebraic procedures. Thus to obtain a general factor in the factor analysis of items is not as impressive a demonstration as might first appear. Rotation, on the other hand, as was shown in Chapter 5, takes variance from the general factor and redistributes it. However, this is contrary to what is required in item factor analysis. The best way around this difficulty is to develop several scales at once, as for example in a personality inventory such as the EPQ measuring extraversion, anxiety and psychoticism. Then rotation to simple structure or even confirmatory analysis makes sense.

6 All these problems mean that the correlations between items are highly unreliable. To minimize this it is necessary to use large samples and to have as large a subject to variables ratio as is possible. Since in test construction it is usual to write at least twice as many items as are required in the test, so that only items loading highly on the test are selected, this means that subject numbers are big. To try out the 200 items necessary for a five variable test (20 items per scale) a sample of 1,000 subjects would be desirable. This is often difficult to obtain unless large resources are available.

Conclusions

With so many problems many test constructors have used different methods and these will be briefly described. A full discussion can be found in Kline (1992).

Item analysis

A set of trial items is administered to a sample. The essence of item analysis is the correlation of each item with the total score. Items which correlate the most highly with the total score are selected on the grounds that these are measuring what most of the items are measuring. Thus the set of items so selected ought to be virtually identical to the set of items loading on the general factor. In addition a further criterion for item selection is that the correct answer should be obtained by 20–80 per cent of the sample. This rules out undiscriminating items.

Because only correlations (of items with the total score) are used in item analysis, that these correlations are unreliable is not so important as in factor analysis, which attempts to reproduce the correlations. It is also less necessary to use huge samples. Indeed, Nunnally (1978) advocates that item analysis be used to make the first item selection and then the items be factored.

Although item analysis usually gives similar results to factor analysis, there are conditions in which it is not so effective. Thus if we have a set of items in which there are two correlated factors, item analysis will select items loading on either or both and thus an unsatisfactory test will be produced. In personality test development where writing items is something of an art and it is difficult to tell what they measure this is a real difficulty.

Two other methods of test construction are used which I shall mention extremely briefly because they have a different rationale and are in no way to be seen as substitutes for factor analysis.

Criterion keyed tests

In these tests items are selected from a pool if they discriminate a criterion group, e.g. alcoholics, from controls. However, such tests suffer from the problem that groups differ on many variables so that the resulting set of items will not be unifactorial and thus their psychological meaning will be dubious. These tests are suitable only for screening purposes, as in large-scale selection procedures.

Tests based on item characteristic curves

The characteristic curve of an item indicates the probability of individuals' different levels of the latent trait (e.g. intelligence in an intelligence test) putting the correct response. On the basis of such curves and with models of item response it is possible to construct tests with sets of exactly equivalent items. However, assumptions have to be made about the latent traits underlying the items and these methods are usually only suitable for tests of ability and attainment. For further discussion see Kline (1992).

From this discussion it is clear that despite the problems involved factor analysis is the best method of test construction since, as our model of test variance made clear, essentially what is required is a unifactorial test.

Before examining some examples of factor analyses in test construction there is one further problem which is conceptual rather than technical but which infirms much test construction especially in social psychology.

The bloated specific in test construction

A good test has items which load a common factor. The higher the loading the better the test. However, if we write items which are virtual paraphrases of each other they will correlate highly and load on a common factor. An example will clarify the point. Suppose that we are constructing a test of extraversion, of which one of the characteristics is liking a noisy exciting time. We might write the following items.

1 I like noisy parties.
2 I really enjoy an evening in a pub with a crowd of people.
3 I just like being in a group of people.
4 I like lively, noisy groups.
5 I love talking and joking with a crowd of friends.
6 I hate being on my own.
7 I can't just sit and do nothing.
8 I enjoy a quiet evening reading.
9 I like browsing round a quiet library or museum.

It would not be surprising if these items were highly correlated and formed a factor. However, it might well be nothing more than a bloated specific concerned with responding to items involving noise. This, of course, demonstrates that, in test construction, it is not sufficient to demonstrate that items load a factor. It is also necessary to show what that factor is. To do this the test would have to be validated against external criteria or located in factor space as was fully discussed in Chapter 7. Indeed this is the empirical distinction between a common factor and a bloated specific. A common factor will correlate with or discriminate among external criteria. A bloated specific by definition correlates with nothing.

EXAMPLES OF FACTOR ANALYSIS IN TEST CONSTRUCTION

The construction of the PPQ (Kline and Lapham 1991)

Aim of the study

This study reported the results of an attempt to construct a personality questionnaire, the PPQ, which measured the five factors currently regarded as accounting for much of the variance in personality questionnaires. These factors, although sometimes given different names, are extraversion, confidence (the other pole of anxiety), openness to experience, tough mindedness and conscientiousness. The test was designed, it should be added, to be suited for occupational selection.

General description of the method

We intended to factor analyse a set of items in order to extract five clear factors. Items were written to measure each factor. To speed the process and to reduce the number of subjects required for a first trial these were factored separately, e.g. the extraversion set and the conscientiousness set. Items were selected for each factor which loaded that factor and correlated with the total score using item analysis, as described above. Items which showed sex differences were also rejected.

All these items, having been initially selected, were then subjected to a simple structure factor analysis. The resulting PPQ scales were then factored with the EPQ in a study of their validity.

Sample

A total of 1,472 students in four large universities completed the test (906 females and 566 males).

Factor analysis

As discussed throughout this book, we used the most efficient method for obtaining simple structure – principal components, Scree test, rotation of significant factors by Direct Oblimin.

Comments on the method

The items were intercorrelated using Pearson correlations (algebraically identical with ϕ) and principal components were used rather than factors because in a matrix of this size the differences between factors and components would be negligible, certainly as regards the main factors of the matrix.

The sample is sufficiently large to be representative of the student population, being drawn from the main faculties, and to reduce the standard errors of the correlations between the items to negligible proportions.

A confirmatory analysis might have seemed preferable to a simple structure rotation but with so large a sample we argued that it would be difficult to confirm our hypothetical five factors. Thus simple structure seemed to be a more powerful test.

Results

The results are set out in Table 8.1. First it should be noted that for simplicity we only show the items which were actually included in the final version of the PPQ. Again for brevity and clarity I shall discuss points under separate heads.

Table 8.1 Structure matrix of a five factor Direct Oblimin rotation of a principal components solution

	Factor 1 (Convention)	Factor 2 (Conscience)	Factor 3 (Insecurity)	Factor 4 (Tender)	Factor 5 (Introversion)
Q44	−0.621	−0.095	−0.182	0.079	−0.118
Q55	−0.599	−0.219	−0.117	0.131	−0.093
Q100	0.596	0.215	0.214	−0.112	0.077
Q41	−0.572	−0.193	−0.220	0.012	−0.120
Q83	0.565	0.353	0.328	0.008	0.110
Q75	0.450	0.347	0.334	0.044	0.067
Q73	−0.441	−0.213	−0.248	0.081	−0.123
Q89	−0.435	−0.207	−0.003	−0.098	−0.122
Q51	0.390	0.217	0.105	0.046	0.060
Q36	−0.334	−0.073	0.217	0.227	0.184
Q60	0.305	0.235	0.188	0.168	0.021
Q47	−0.283	0.102	0.191	−0.131	−0.155
Q91	−0.248	−0.067	−0.166	0.073	−0.187
Q98	−0.237	−0.197	−0.181	0.062	−0.178
Q3	−0.216	−0.174	−0.106	0.094	0.044
Q23	0.232	0.651	−0.020	−0.092	0.007
Q86	0.204	0.648	0.089	−0.093	0.027
Q7	0.078	0.593	−0.062	−0.078	0.118
Q69	−0.093	−0.575	0.073	0.082	−0.094
Q62	0.086	0.523	−0.008	0.011	−0.029
Q93	0.205	0.501	0.114	−0.002	−0.139
Q20	0.313	0.494	0.121	−0.058	0.122
Q88	0.354	0.472	−0.015	−0.142	−0.081
Q53	−0.133	−0.434	0.016	−0.069	−0.030
Q65	0.135	0.391	0.223	−0.188	−0.154
Q4	−0.221	−0.381	0.066	−0.010	0.072
Q16	−0.113	−0.351	−0.032	0.004	0.116
Q50	0.120	0.343	0.082	−0.095	0.091
Q59	0.099	0.128	0.631	0.134	0.046
Q77	0.001	0.075	0.600	−0.040	−0.024
Q57	−0.162	0.065	−0.570	−0.119	−0.115
Q67	0.085	0.031	0.599	0.333	0.280
Q85	−0.157	0.144	−0.508	0.005	−0.197
Q43	−0.004	0.051	−0.490	0.024	0.024
Q33	0.061	0.001	0.477	−0.039	0.119

(cont.)

Q34	−0.90	0.089	−0.469	−0.375	−0.327
Q74	0.162	0.271	0.469	−0.012	0.142
Q99	0.046	−0.010	0.460	0.375	0.278
Q24	−0.174	−0.069	−0.376	0.016	−0.245
Q92	0.221	0.342	0.350	−0.004	0.176
Q72	−0.148	0.003	−0.334	−0.046	−0.151
Q38	−0.45	0.096	−0.289	0.265	0.154
Q28	−0.085	−0.179	0.235	−0.028	0.234
Q64	−0.019	−0.124	−0.046	0.671	0.188
Q25	0.020	0.127	0.024	−0.664	−0.184
Q94	0.021	−0.026	0.058	0.539	0.187
Q61	0.029	0.037	−0.106	−0.522	−0.095
Q21	0.022	0.025	0.075	0.462	0.119
Q80	−0.055	−0.008	−0.203	−0.454	−0.255
Q5	−0.039	0.184	0.128	−0.425	−0.163
Q63	−0.046	0.258	0.107	−0.386	−0.261
Q96	0.326	0.283	0.050	−0.385	0.044
Q19	−0.352	−0.208	0.002	0.360	−0.037
Q70	−0.216	−0.003	0.103	0.266	−0.034
Q78	0.059	0.006	0.178	−0.217	−0.073
Q48	−0.035	−0.026	−0.116	−0.359	−0.632
Q82	−0.114	−0.032	−0.119	−0.061	−0.622
Q76	0.149	0.017	0.053	0.108	0.606
Q37	−0.162	0.086	0.035	−0.106	−0.586
Q6	0.015	0.038	0.148	0.295	0.545
Q26	0.066	0.153	0.189	0.037	0.545
Q18	−0.104	0.187	−0.098	−0.266	−0.442
Q79	0.084	−0.151	−0.309	−0.238	−0.439
Q40	0.081	0.316	−0.081	−0.398	−0.436
Q15	−0.215	0.074	−0.190	−0.250	−0.395
Q14	−0.315	−0.046	0.008	−0.164	−0.318
Q2	0.182	0.202	0.187	0.123	0.311
Q68	0.148	0.137	0.084	0.203	0.244
Alpha	0.73	0.78	0.76	0.70	0.76

Note: $n = 1,472$.

1 It is quite clear that there are five factors in this set of items.
However, the factor structure of these items is not as simple as is
desirable. Thus in factor 1 four of the items load less than 0.3 on
the factor. Although this correlation is significant, higher loadings would be preferred. Some items not on this factor, e.g.
Q88, load more highly than the items on this factor. This is
because an item is selected for a factor by its highest loading.
This has some undesirable consequences.

2 An ideal criterion for selecting an item for a test is that it loads
one factor only. This produces a unifactorial test. However, if

we examine the items in factor 1 we can see that this has not been entirely achieved. For example, item Q83 has loadings greater than 0.3 on factors 2 and 3. This item loads these factors more highly than some of the items on those factors. Indeed many of the items do not load only one factor.

Examination of the factor matrix indicates that even these selected items do not only load one factor. Given that this is contrary to the ideal criterion it is reasonable to ask why these items were selected. The answer to this is simple. The other items, not included in the matrix, were worse. They either had even higher loadings on other factors or they loaded on none. These items load their scales and do not load highly on others. They are far from perfect but, it is hoped, not too bad.

3 As might be expected from the item loadings these factors were correlated. However, the correlations were moderate, the largest being that between conventionality and conscientiousness (0.417), a finding which supports the validity of these scales since both these traits are part of the syndrome of the obsessional personality.

4 As has been seen this is not a bad five factor structure even though it is not perfect. As was mentioned above confirmatory analysis was rejected on the grounds that any loosely specified target matrix would be too easy to fit even with so large a sample. Examination of Table 8.1 shows clearly the truth of this assertion because all items would have one large loading and all the rest zero. Thus this is not a sufficiently specified matrix to make confirmatory analysis effective, even without the problems of the huge sample.

Validity of the factors

In test construction even if factors are obtained it is necessary to demonstrate what those factors are. To investigate the validity of the factors a second study of the kind discussed in the previous chapter was conducted.

Sample A sample of 100 students (44 female, 56 male) from two large universities was used.

Tests The PPQ and EPQ tests were used, measuring extraversion, anxiety and psychoticism plus a social desirability scale.

Factor analysis of the correlations between the scales A Direct Oblimin simple structure analysis of the principal components analysis was carried out. A Scree test showed that there were three factors and the results are set out in Table 8.2.

Table 8.2 Structure matrix of a three factor Direct Oblimin rotation of a principal components solution for PPQ and EPQ scale scores

		Factor 1	*Factor 2*	*Factor 3*
PPQ	Insecure	0.803	0.008	−0.238
EPQ	Extravert	−0.725	0.064	0.107
PPQ	Introvert	0.716	−0.194	−0.463
EPQ	Neuroticism	0.652	0.052	0.244
PPQ	Convention	0.606	0.545	−0.378
PPQ	Conscience	0.194	0.739	−0.372
PPQ	Tender	0.380	−0.702	−0.248
EPQ	Social desirability	0.118	0.162	−0.742
EPQ	Psychotic	−0.112	−0.048	0.739

Note: $n = 100$.

Comments   I shall say little about the design of this study which was an exploratory analysis to locate the PPQ factors relative to those in the EPQ. The methods used are identical to those discussed in the last chapter.

These factors accounted for 62 per cent of the variance and to some extent support the validity of the PPQ, but it is not a clear solution and has some extraordinary features. Thus factor 1 loads both EPQ anxiety and introversion. These, however, are supposed to be independent factors. Factor 2 is probably the authoritarian factor, as discussed in Chapter 7, with its loadings on conventionality, tender-mindedness and conscientiousness. Factor 3 seems to be one of social desirability and the loadings indicate the extent to which the scales are affected by the tendency to respond in a socially desirable fashion.

It must be noted that the PPQ scales are not entirely factor pure. Thus conventionality loads all three factors, as to a lesser extent do conscientiousness and tender-mindedness. However, the meaning of this factor analysis relative to the validity of the scales is hard to interpret because of the fact that anxiety and introversion load the same factor.

Conclusions

This factor analysis of the items in the PPQ and the subsequent factoring of the scales with the Eysenck scales is not conclusive. It has shown that there are five factors in the PPQ but these do not seem as independent as might be hoped. Furthermore the factor analysis with the EPQ was surprising and difficult to clarify. The PPQ requires considerably more research before it could be accepted as a valid test of the big five factors and ideally some more items should be constructed and factored with it to increase the length and independence of the scales.

From the viewpoint of seeing how factor analysis can be used in test construction, these results are highly useful since they demonstrate the difficulty of producing factor pure scales and show how even when these scales have been produced their place in factor space is not necessarily what might have been expected.

The EPQ: a study by Hashemi (1981)

Sometimes the factor structure of the items is not quoted in the manual to the test, even though it was constructed by factor analysis. In this case the structure can be examined *post hoc*. This was done by Hashemi (1981) and in this example I shall examine some of the results which he obtained in his outstanding thesis.

I shall present a simplified version of the results to make the necessary points about the use of factor analysis in test construction. It must be borne in mind that the aim of these analyses is to produce a set of items which load highly only on one factor. As was made clear from the first example this is a difficult ideal to attain: with that test the items loaded some other factors as well and some of the factor loadings were small.

Subjects

Hashemi (1981) examined four samples – one from a previous study by Helmes, and referred to under that name, and three other samples: a Thai student sample ($N = 116$), a British student sample ($N = 406$) and an adult Gallup sample ($N = 1,198$). There were no important sex differences in this study so I shall deal with the results from the combined samples.

Factor analysis

The item correlations in each sample were subjected to principal components analysis and four factors (their being four scales in the EPQ), despite the Scree and Velicer (1976) MAP tests which indicated more factors, were rotated to simple structure using Direct Oblimin.

Results

Table 8.3 shows the number and percentage of items with their highest loadings on their keyed scale and Table 8.4 shows the mean loadings of scale items.

Table 8.3 Number and percentage of items with their highest loading on keyed scale

Scale	Number of items	Helmes Promax/Varimax	Thai students	British students	British adults
P	25	14 (56%)	10 (40%)	21 (84%)	25 (100%)
E	21	16 (76%)/17 (81%) 17 (81%)	19 (90%)	20 (95%)	21 (100%)
N	23	22 (96%)	20 (87%)	23 (100%)	23 (100%)
L	21	18 (86%)	18 (86%)	19 (90%)	21 (100%)

Table 8.4 Mean absolute factor loading of scale items

Scale	Helmes (Procrustes)	Thai students	British students	British adults
P	0.255	0.167	0.333	0.390
E	0.455	0.401	0.516	0.511
N	0.472	0.388	0.462	0.506
L	0.377	0.374	0.374	0.429

Comments

It will be noted that Hashemi rotated fewer factors than were suggested by the extraction tests. As was discussed in Chapter 5, underfactoring tends to telescope factors together and to *produce second-order factors at the first order*. However, the Eysenck factors E,

N, P and L are second order and so this underfactoring was, in this instance, an effective method of factoring these data. In any case these loadings were compared with a previous study in which the EPQ items had been factored and there was an extremely close agreement.

Table 8.3 indicates that the majority of items, with the exception of P, loaded their scales. Although I do not include these figures Hashemi found that the loadings of these items on their other factors were small. Indeed the quality of these items should be judged from the extremely large Gallup sample where all the items loaded up, exactly as they should. It is to be noted that this Gallup sample is not only large, thus minimizing the standard errors of the correlations and increasing thereby the accuracy of the factor analysis, but in addition it was chosen to be representative of the adult population rather than simply students.

In all cases the results obtained with the Thai students are the least good but this is hardly surprising since tests rarely work as effectively in populations different from those for which they were designed. What is interesting is not that the results are not as good as with the larger British samples but that they are as good as they are.

There can be little doubt that from the factor analytic viewpoint the EPQ is a truly impressive test with the items loading up as about as efficiently as could be expected. Again it must be reiterated that this does not mean that the test is valid only that it has a clear four factor structure.

Examination of Table 8.4 is also informative. From this it is clear that the average factor loadings of these items on their factors was satisfactorily high. The weakest factor in both tables was the P factor. Examination of the item splits revealed the cause of this – namely that in the Gallup sample nine of the P items were endorsed by less than 20 per cent of the sample and in the case of the females (the only important sex difference) this proportion was even higher. It is interesting to note that in the new version of the EPQ, the EPQR, this problem has been remedied by the addition of some new items.

Finally I want to say a brief word about the Helmes results. These were not as good as those of Hashemi and this Hashemi attributes to imperfect methodology. Thus Helmes rotated too many factors (eigenvalues greater than 1). As we have seen in Chapter 5, Promax and Varimax are not as efficient as Direct

Oblimin at reaching simple structure. Finally, in computing the item loadings on the second-order factors Helmes used a method which is not the most effective, although this is a more technical issue than I want to discuss at this point. In brief the Helmes results were due to technical imperfections although it should be said that the EPQ does not emerge from that study as a bad test.

Conclusions

This study by Hashemi (1981) demonstrates clearly the effectiveness of factor analysis in test construction. Although this was a published test, if these items had been administered to these samples in a test trial we would have selected them on the strength of their factor loadings. The one weak factor (among normals it must be stressed) has been corrected and this weakness was detected in the factor analysis.

CONCLUSIONS

I shall not give any further examples in this chapter of factor analysis in test construction since these two factor analyses illustrate the main points. Nevertheless it is worth summarizing the most salient issues since these are often forgotten in factoring test items.

1 The difficulty of correlating dichotomous items does lead to factors of small variance. Large samples are therefore necessary for reliable results.
2 Attempts to overcome this difficulty by analysing groups of items rather than individual items, item parcels to use Cattell's (1978) terminology, tend to lead to second-order factors. Barrett and Kline (1982) used this method in their study of the 16PF test in which the items as well as item parcels were factored. Neither method yielded 16 factors despite the fact that samples were large and various methods of factor analysis were used in an effort to reach simple structure.
3 It is necessary, as was clear from the first example, to select as far as is possible items which load only on one factor.
4 It is best to have an as high as possible criterion of factor loadings for retaining items. Again this is difficult but 0.3 would appear to be a sensible minimum, although often lower values have to be accepted. I believe that this was the weakness in the construction

of the 16PF test, i.e. that too low loadings were accepted, although admittedly statistically significant.

5 Factors must be identified by more than the items loading on them.

6 Hashemi (1981) both factored and item analysed the EPQ in the Thai sample. He found virtually perfect agreement between the two methods. Thus the same items would have been excluded by item and by factor analysis and the items ranked by factor loadings and by correlations with the total score were almost identical.

7 It is best, because of the algebra of factor analysis, to construct several scales at once and rotate to simple structure.

8 Confirmatory analysis, because of the problems of the χ^2 test with large samples and the necessary crudity of the target matrix, is not really a sensible method, despite its statistical qualities, in test construction (but see Chapter 10 where this matter is further discussed).

One final point needs to be made clear. In this examination of factor analysis in test construction I have not once mentioned the test content. This does not mean that it is unimportant and that all that matters is an efficient factor analysis. This would be nonsensical. A test can be no better than its items. What a test measures depends entirely on its items and factor analysis essentially sorts them into groups. However, this book is concerned with factor analysis. How items should be written is fully discussed in Kline (1992).

From all these arguments it is clear that with sufficiently large samples factor analysis is an effective method of test construction, given that the constraints and limitations, discussed in this chapter, are taken into account.

Chapter 9

Factor analysis in a wider context

In Chapters 7 and 8 we have seen examples of factor analysis used for somewhat specific purposes. In Chapter 7 we saw that by factoring a test with the main personality and ability factors and by rotation to simple structure its place in factor space could be determined. This effectively demonstrated what it measured and such factor analytic designs are powerful in test validation. Since the majority of tests are not valid this is an important aspect of psychological measurement.

In Chapter 8 we discussed two examples of factor analytic test construction. Its advantages and problems became evident and in many respects it was shown to be an ideal method of test construction. Nevertheless the dangers of merely producing a bloated specific of items which are little more than paraphrases of each other were stressed along with the necessity of validating any item factors.

Factor analysis can be used for more general purposes in psychology and the social sciences. It can elegantly answer questions which if other methods were used would be exceedingly cumbrous. In this chapter I shall illustrate these broader capabilities of factor analysis. My examples will not cover all the social sciences but I shall choose those where the application to quite different fields is easy to see and these extensions will be discussed.

In some ways this broader approach and application of factor analysis is more interesting and potentially of greater value for research than the more conventional uses which have been discussed in the previous chapters. However, it has to be said that these wider uses are far more rare.

EXAMPLE 1: A STUDY OF THE PSYCHOSOCIAL CHARACTERISTICS OF LONG-TERM TRANQUILLIZER USERS (PICKERING 1986)

Background and aim of the research

The problem of long-term users of tranquillizers, especially the benzodiazepines, of which Valium is the best known, has recently been highlighted. This study sought to examine the characteristics, psychological and social, of a group of patients in a general practice who had been taking these drugs for three months or longer. If such patients could be differentiated it would be useful for the general practitioner who could then recognize the probability that they would become 'addicted' and act accordingly. This is not difficult since it is generally recognized that any therapeutic effects of the benzodiazepines become less and less with prolonged use.

Sample

A random sample of long-term users in a general practice was selected ($N = 103$: 34 men, 69 women). As was usual there were more men than women in this group. These were compared with controls selected from the practice list and matched for sex, age and social class.

Variables

1 The General Health Questionnaire (Goldberg 1978), measuring the current state of subjects' psychiatric well-being.
2 Cattell's 16PF test measuring primary personality factors.
3 The Life Events Schedule (Paykel and Mangen 1980), administered by a semi-structured interview and designed to assess the impact of various life events such as deaths and divorces.
4 Certain data from the medical records, e.g. whether patients were suffering from chronic illness and number of referrals, were collected as were ratings of the patients' general health and relationship with the doctor.

From these measures the following variables were analysed, as set out in Table 9.1.

Table 9.1 Key to variables

SOH	Size of household
CAH	Number of children living at home
FAM	Size of family of origin
CHUR	Churchgoing
JS	'Job' satisfaction
NCF	Number of close friends
CONF	Ability to confide
PRGH	Patient rating of own general health
PRAC	Patient rating of own health as a child
SMOK	Regular smoking
ALC	Regular consumption of alcohol
NPD	Regular non-prescribed drugs
DAC	Doctor for non-medical problems
DID	Doctor if depressed
RWDA	Patient rating of relationship with doctor
ANG	Ability to express anger
DPC	Number of doctor–patient contacts in one year
REF	Number of referrals to other agencies during one year
REP	Number of repeat prescriptions during one year
DRGH	Doctor rating of general health
DRR	Doctor rating of doctor–patient relationship
TOL	Time on doctor's list
CMC	Chronic medical condition (if any)
GHQ	General Health Questionnaire score
LIFE	Life Events Schedule score
A–Q4	Personality traits (measured by 16 PF questionnaire)

Factor analysis

Principal components analysis was computed followed by the Scree test which selected five factors. Principal factors were computed and five factors were rotated to simple structure using Direct Oblimin.

Comments on the factor analytic design

A more usual design, given that the aim was to study the psychosocial characteristics of a group, would be analysis of variance or discriminant function analysis between the two groups. However, factor analysis is an exceedingly neat and elegant answer to these questions. Thus all variables which significantly loaded the factor on which the dummy variable experimental group (1 or 0) loaded would be discriminating for that group.

Results

Table 9.2 sets out the results of the oblique factor analysis.

Table 9.2 Direct Oblimin rotation of factors

	Factor					
	1	2	3	4	5	*Communality*
Q4	*0.851*	0.073	−0.260	0.149	0.224	(0.802)
C	*−0.828*	−0.010	0.219	0.050	−0.270	(0.726)
O	*0.823*	0.102	−0.214	0.189	0.222	(0.755)
CONTRL	*−0.730*	−0.037	0.107	−0.179	*−0.448*	(0.641)
DRR	*0.546*	0.037	−0.009	−0.055	0.181	(0.303)
DPC	*0.529*	−0.015	−0.060	0.060	*0.409*	(0.367)
RWDA	*0.511*	0.056	−0.113	−0.035	0.033	(0.279)
H	*−0.492*	−0.121	*0.485*	−0.224	−0.274	(0.513)
Q3	*−0.484*	−0.000	−0.203	*0.326*	−0.078	(0.368)
N	*0.443*	0.108	−0.051	−0.148	0.268	(0.259)
L	*0.430*	0.034	0.111	0.129	0.116	(0.228)
NCF	*−0.416*	−0.185	0.138	0.138	−0.248	(0.260)
NPD	*0.367*	0.015	0.008	0.111	0.114	(0.152)
GHQ	*0.335*	0.040	0.055	−0.017	0.139	(0.122)
DID	0.222	0.003	−0.112	−0.131	−0.080	(0.093)
ALC	0.168	−0.086	0.144	−0.133	−0.109	(0.088)
CONF	−0.040	*0.960*	−0.075	−0.099	−0.003	(0.947)
CMC	−0.126	*0.945*	−0.023	−0.081	−0.007	(0.938)
CAH	−0.061	*0.852*	0.149	−0.030	−0.246	(0.823)
SOH	−0.047	*0.788*	0.189	0.033	−0.270	(0.750)
JS	*0.310*	*0.687*	−0.054	−0.166	0.196	(0.603)
ANG	0.288	*0.664*	−0.192	0.058	0.216	(0.550)
Q2	0.216	−0.002	*−0.744*	−0.002	0.097	(0.605)
F	−0.250	−0.083	*0.702*	−0.165	−0.230	(0.569)
M	−0.106	−0.119	*−0.596*	−0.110	−0.161	(0.444)
A	−0.177	−0.044	*0.514*	−0.040	−0.168	(0.298)
I	−0.213	0.020	*−0.503*	0.217	−0.094	(0.346)
SMOK	0.150	−0.022	0.170	−0.097	0.063	(0.062)
G	−0.014	0.007	−0.204	*0.678*	0.157	(0.483)
Q1	0.222	−0.084	0.175	*−0.654*	−0.400	(0.540)
E	−0.112	−0.092	*0.426*	*−0.516*	−0.209	(0.436)
CHUR	−0.004	−0.032	−0.085	*0.381*	0.072	(0.150)
TOL	0.034	−0.065	−0.023	0.275	0.153	(0.094)
FAM	−0.009	−0.074	0.080	0.268	−0.016	(0.092)
DAC	−0.081	−0.064	0.015	−0.092	0.014	(0.022)
PRGH	0.262	−0.006	−0.032	0.061	*0.745*	(0.564)

(cont.)

DRGH	−0.002	−0.003	−0.044	0.053	*0.646*	(0.448)
REF	*0.488*	0.022	0.007	0.066	*0.530*	(0.422)
REP	*0.341*	0.013	−0.042	0.169	*0.461*	(0.283)
B	−0.105	−0.058	−0.161	*−0.363*	−0.384	(0.292)
PRAC	0.277	0.014	−0.111	0.081	*0.362*	(0.177)
LIFE	0.022	−0.043	−0.010	0.081	0.128	(0.022)
Eigenvalue	6.744	4.243	2.690	2.062	1.253	

Comments

Before these factors can be interpreted the correlations should be noted. The only one that was not trivial was the negative correlation of −0.242 between factors 1 and 5.

Factor 1

This is the critical factor. This discriminates the control and experimental group highly with its loading of 0.730. Clearly every variable which loads on this factor is involved in the discrimination of the tranquillizer and the control group, which, it must be remembered, are closely matched.

The highest loadings are on the Cattell factors Q4, C and O, which are all above 0.8. These are all the primary factors of the Cattell anxiety factor. With the utmost clarity this factor 1 has revealed that the tranquillizer users are more neurotic or anxious than the controls. These loadings refer to the trait of anxiety, not the transient state anxiety, which has a definite causal basis. In addition they have more neurotic symptoms than controls, as measured by the GHQ. Even if this is not surprising it confirms the power of the factor analytic approach in this study.

Other variables discriminating the groups are highly revealing. Thus the long-term tranquillizer users may be described as suspicious (L), timid (H−) and with poor emotional control (Q3−). In addition they have few close friends. Medical variables are also implicated. Thus they have more referrals to other agencies and more repeat prescriptions than do the controls (although this latter point must reflect, to some extent, their use of tranquillizers). Similarly they differ from controls in respect of the doctor's rating of their relationship, and tend to use more non-prescribed drugs.

This factor 1 tells us a good deal about long-term tranquillizer users. They are highly neurotic and with some degree of psychiatric symptoms. It is typical of such a group that they have been referred comparatively often to other agencies.

In a study of this kind, what variables do not load a factor can be as informative as variables that do. For example, going to church or being satisfied with one's job have no relation to the long-term consumption of benzodiazepines. Similarly, life events were not related.

This is an exploratory study. These loadings all provide hypotheses which should be examined in further detail both in this sample and in other studies. It should be pointed out that this was, in fact, done by Pickering (1986) in her thesis. Nevertheless, even without this information, there is no doubt that this factor 1 is highly informative.

In brief this factor 1 has shown that tranquilliser users are more anxious and display more psychiatric symptoms than controls. They have not been more involved in traumatic life events than controls nor have they less job satisfaction. Furthermore they differ from controls in respect of their relationship with the doctor and in that they have been referred to other agencies to a greater extent. They would appear to be an anxious group who use their general practitioners as a way of dealing with their difficulties.

Factor 5

The other relevant factor in this study is factor 5 since group membership loaded -0.448 on it. Examination of its high loadings suggests that this is a 'patient' factor, a factor concerned with variables that relate to being or playing the role of a patient, a common phenomenon in the surgeries of the general practitioner. This interpretation is supported by the loadings on patient's rating of own health, the doctor rating of the general health of the patient, the fact that they had been referred to other agencies and that they have had repeat prescriptions. This last, however, as has been argued, may be part and parcel of long-term tranquillizer use. Finally it should be noted that the tranquillizer group were less intelligent (factor B) than the controls.

Again this factor 5 is revealing. The long-term user of these drugs seems himself or herself as a patient and the prescription of these drugs supports this role.

Finally it must be stressed that these factor analytic interpretations must be regarded as hypotheses to be put to the test in more detailed examinations of the data and in further studies. Nevertheless this research by Pickering (1986) is a good example of how factor analysis can be useful in the study of quite broad questions in the social sciences.

EXAMPLE 2: Q FACTOR ANALYSIS IN THE STUDY OF OFFENDERS (HAMPSON 1975)

In this investigation three small samples of offenders who were legally classified as 'mentally abnormal' were given a battery of personality tests, questionnaires and projective tests. Four samples of controls matched for age, sex, IQ and institutionalization were also tested.

The questions asked in this investigation concerned the nature of abnormal offenders, whether they might be discriminated from controls in terms of personality traits and whether there were subgroups of offenders. To answer this the data were subjected to Q factor analysis. As was pointed out in Chapter 5 Q factor analyses makes use of the same data as the regular R analyses with which we have been concerned up to now. However, unlike R analysis, in Q analysis subjects, not variables, are correlated and the resulting factors load on subjects. These Q factors, therefore, define groups. In subsequent analyses of the data the variables discriminating these factorially defined groups can be studied.

Subjects

Fifteen male offenders detained in mental hospitals for such offences as arson, indecent assault, assault and theft were tested.

Comparison groups

Nine students (a pilot study); ten males from a training centre for abnormals; and 14 marines were used as comparison groups.

Tests

1 Projective measures: Porteus mazes, Pinman recall test, family relations indicator (FRI), Thematic Apperception Test (TAT), house tree person (HTP) test.
2 Questionnaires: 16PF, Eysenck personality inventory, Eysenck

Withers personality inventory (offenders), dynamic personality inventory, sensation seeking scale and the conservatism scale.

In the pilot study all these tests were given to offenders and the comparison group. However, the projective tests were far better than the questionnaires at discriminating the offenders and the projective tests were used alone in the subsequent studies.

Scoring the projective tests

These tests were subjected to a content analysis in which features were either present or absent (1 or 0) in a subject's protocol. This dichotomous scoring system is highly reliable, thus overcoming one of the main weaknesses of projective tests. Only variables on which at least five subjects scored 1 were retained, leaving 119 variables.

Q factor analysis

Three separate studies were carried out in which the offenders were factored with each comparison group. Subjects were correlated using the G index, a special correlation coefficient which has been shown to be suited to factor analysis (Holley and Guilford 1964). These correlations were subjected to principal components analysis and all factors with eigenvalues greater than 1 were rotated to simple structure using a Promax oblique rotation. As was argued in Chapters 4 and 5 this factor analytic procedure is far from ideal. However, it has to be pointed out that at Exeter, at the time of this study, Promax was the only oblique rotation available. Eigenvalues greater than unity were used here rather than the Scree test because compression of factors, thus forcing subjects into groups, was not considered sensible. That there might be too many factors was not a serious defect.

Results

The three Q factor analyses are set out in Tables 9.3, 9.4 and 9.5.

Table 9.3 Offender subgroup factors in analysis 1

Subjects	Factor 1	Factor 2
1	−0.06	0.16
2	0.16	0.12
3	−0.10	0.71
4	0.74	0.03
5	0.60	0.08
6	0.28	−0.04
7	0.65	0.25
8	0.48	−0.31
9	0.23	−0.16
10	0.11	0.70
11	0.09	−0.10
12	−0.02	0.31
13	0.32	0.07
14	0.20	0.64
15	−0.05	0.19
16	−0.15	0.08
17	0.09	−0.04
18	−0.27	0.11
19	−0.03	−0.01
20	0.14	0.17
21	0.07	0.11
22	0.09	0.04
23	−0.15	−0.23
24	−0.06	0.07

Comments

The aim of these Q factor analyses was not simply to discriminate the comparison groups from the offenders. For this other techniques such as discriminant functions are more suited. The intention was to discover any groups discriminated in terms of personality among offenders and to see whether these were separate from comparison groups of non-offenders.

Table 9.3 shows the results of the first Promax analysis, the pilot study of offenders and controls. Of the nine factors rotated two, shown in Table 9.2, had high loadings on offenders only. It should be noted that subjects 1–15 are the offenders. These two Q factors indicate that offenders 4, 5, 7, 8 and 13 fall into one group, defined by the projective test scores, while offenders 3, 10, 12 and 14 form another category. Subject 8 has a high negative loading. In Q factoring this appears somewhat strange. However, all it means is that this subject lies at the opposite end of the dimension which

Table 9.4 Offender subgroup factors in analysis 2

Subjects	Factor 1	Factor 2
1	0.23	−0.19
2	−0.15	0.00
3	0.07	*−0.60*
4	*−0.66*	−0.26
5	*−0.55*	−0.03
6	−0.19	0.00
7	*−0.50*	−0.21
8	*−0.56*	0.28
9	−0.12	0.05
10	−0.13	*−0.74*
11	0.03	0.15
12	−0.03	*−0.44*
13	*−0.56*	−0.08
14	−0.10	*−0.69*
15	−0.06	−0.12
16	−0.00	0.09
17	−0.13	−0.17
18	0.16	0.02
19	−0.04	0.00
20	−0.04	0.04
21	−0.11	0.08
22	0.06	−0.28
23	−0.09	0.03
24	−0.13	0.12
25	0.17	−0.16

groups the subjects together on factor 1.

Table 9.4 shows the result of the Q factor analysis with the subnormal group, in which eight factors were subjected to oblique rotation. Again these two offender subgroups load the two factors. In the study with the marines these subjects are again grouped together, although on factor 1 there was an extra offender with a high loading −0.6.

To understand this group the dimension must be identified. This was done by identifying the variables which discriminated the two groups. These are called the characteristic variables and are scrutinized below. This discussion is inevitably a summary of the findings but further details can be found in Hampson (1975) and in Hampson and Kline (1977), which is a brief report of the original thesis. In addition it is interesting to note the offences for which the offenders were convicted. In this way the psychological character-istics of these two offender groups which were stable in all three

Table 9.5 Offender subgroup factors in analysis 3

Subjects	Factor 1	Factor 2
1	0.07	−0.11
2	0.24	−0.12
3	−0.26	*−0.79*
4	*0.90*	−0.07
5	*0.49*	0.00
6	*0.35*	0.18
7	*0.36*	−0.26
8	*0.73*	0.23
9	0.16	−0.00
10	0.09	*−0.82*
11	−0.21	0.11
12	0.02	*−0.52*
13	*0.33*	−0.22
14	0.04	*−0.64*
15	−0.07	−0.13
16	−0.07	0.00
17	−0.17	0.08
18	−0.34	−0.01
19	0.29	−0.02
20	−0.06	−0.00
21	0.03	0.06
22	0.13	−0.04
23	0.03	−0.10
24	−0.19	−0.18
25	0.13	0.11
26	0.03	−0.05
27	0.13	0.00
28	0.21	−0.01
29	0.02	0.14

comparisons should be described.

The offences of those on factor 1 included sexually assaulting children, petty theft and arson. From the characteristic TAT variables they appeared to be naive and in the FRI they presented a picture of a family life which had little interaction between parents and children. The HTP test, based upon the dubious clinical interpretations of the manual, suggested that these were people who felt isolated. The first group therefore might be thought of as socially inadequate, based on the characteristic projective test variables.

The offences of those in the second group were concerned with assault, assault and rape and indecent assault on children. In the characteristic TAT responses there was violence and aggression, picture 6, for example, being seen as a murder. The HTP was highly interesting in that two of this group did not complete the test. This in itself is regarded, in the manual, as evidence of psychopathy. In the FRI there were mentions of violence and unhappiness.

In summary this second group of offenders is seen as aggressive and insecure, possibly psychopathic, an identification which certainly fits their crimes.

It should be pointed out that these groups of offenders have been differentiated from comparison groups of non-offenders and from the other offenders in the sample by Q factor analysis of projective test responses. The groups have been tentatively identified in terms of personality by the projective test responses which best discriminated them. The labels socially inadequate and insecurely aggressive, however, must be treated with extreme caution. More work has to be done to identify these Q factor groups.

In their paper Hampson and Kline (1977) attempted further to identify these factors by obtaining factor scores for the subjects and correlating the factor scores with the questionnaire measures which were also administered. I shall not discuss here the results of this study which are of interest simply from the methodological viewpoint. Thus such a procedure is a useful means of identifying Q factors, although there are severe methodological difficulties in obtaining satisfactory factor scores in Q factor analysis, problems which I shall not examine. In addition, because small samples are usually used in Q factor analysis, such correlations have considerable standard errors.

Conclusions

This study has shown how Q factor analysis can be used to discover groups. The advantage of Q factor analysis compared with cluster analytic methods which are the more obvious technique to categorize subjects into groups is that Q factors can be shown to have equivalent R factors in the data, at least under certain conditions. This implies some sort of generality to the findings which the algorithmic search procedures of cluster analysis can never claim.

EXAMPLE 3: THE PLOWDEN REPORT ON PRIMARY EDUCATION (HMSO 1967)

As part of this report Wiseman and Warburton carried out a factor analytic study of academic success at a primary school which clearly answered a number of questions concerning its determinants. As with the other examples, I shall not discuss this research in detail but shall simply examine its general design which is an outstanding example of how factor analysis can be used to answer broad questions in the social sciences, in this case education.

There is constant discussion over what factors determine educational progress. Is it affected, for example, by class size, the qualifications of teachers, the attitudes of parents, the methods of teaching, the size of the school, the education of parents or by none of these factors?

The factor analysis carried out for the Plowden report was designed to throw light on these broad questions. A large sample of children in the Manchester area were given a large battery of tests and measures. In addition, assessments of the home and parents were made by experienced teachers, trained in research, who visited the homes.

Some examples of the variables will clarify the design of this study and demonstrate the exceptional use of factor analysis, which all too often is a routine procedure.

As measures of academic success, standardized tests of academic achievement in English, reading and maths were used. There were also measures of intelligence – picture intelligence for the 7 year olds and verbal reasoning for the older children. School variables such as class size, whether it was mixed or single sex, aided, voluntary or local authority, qualifications of teachers and location of school were included. Home measures included type of house, social class of parents, attitude to education and number of books in the household. Incidentally it is an interesting commentary of the book-buying habits of that period and place that this variable could be satisfactorily measured by the scale 0, 1, 2, more than 2.

All these measures were subjected to a simple structure factor analysis and the determinants of academic success at the primary school were discovered by examining all those variables which loaded on the factor or factors (for there could well be more than one, as will be discussed below) on which the measures of academic success loaded.

I have described this design as exceptional because it is so elegant a solution to a truly difficult problem in which so many variables appear to be involved. I shall simply point out what I consider to be its most important features.

1 The inclusion of all types of variable in the analysis, covering home and school, allows the importance of these to be assessed. It is the wide coverage of variables which makes the research so powerful. This is truly an exploratory design although the inclusion of variables had a definite theoretical basis, namely that family influences were important. Of course, with no theory at all, there is an infinity of possible variables. However, given the practicalities of the research and the questions it was intended to ask there is a broad range of variables.

2 Indeed this is the design which influenced the design of the first example in this chapter, which, on a lesser scale, and to answer quite different questions in a different field, also included a wide range of variables.

3 In the previous section I argued that this design revealed the determinants of academic success. These were the variables loading on the academic success factor or factors. It must be noticed that it was not assumed, in this design, that there would be one factor of academic success. It could be the case that one set of determinants was important for success generally but that a further set were influential for maths. If this were so there would be a separate factor loading on maths alone of the achievement test and on the variables influencing it.

4 I have already argued that this factor analysis is an outstanding example of the genre. However, because it was designed to answer specific practical questions posed by the government of the day, it could be improved, at least in principle. Thus it is likely that personality and motivational variables, i.e. the personal characteristics of the pupils, play some part in their academic success. However, it should be noted that only intelligence tests were used in this study, although ideally measures of personality and motivation would have been included. In practice these are not easy to measure at the primary school age but in an investigation with older children such tests would be highly interesting. Again the influence of such vari-

ables would be shown in the size of their factor loadings on the academic success factor or factors.

5 My interest in this factor analysis in the Plowden report lies in the method which illustrates how it can answer broad questions far beyond the studies of test validity in Chapter 7, vitally important as these are in any scientific endeavour. Nevertheless the results should be briefly mentioned. Thus the highest loading variable on the academic success factor was the intelligence test scores, but crime in the family, the presence or absence of nits in their hair and inadequate cleanliness of the home also loaded highly. This was taken by the authors to indicate, in the light of the other loadings on this factor, that maternal care and parental attitudes were highly influential in academic success at the primary school.

As always in factor analysis, it is equally interesting to note what does not load the relevant factors. For example, class size, contrary to the views of teachers, did not load the factor of academic success highly, having only the moderate loading of 0.36. This would suggest that class size is not an important determinant in academic achievement at the primary school.

I have taken this variable as an example because it illustrates both the power of factor analysis and the care which has to be taken in interpreting the results. Thus, as was suggested above, at first glance the failure to load highly suggests that class size plays no part in the determination of academic success. However, several provisos are required before the full implications can be understood.

1 In this urban sample, the smaller class sizes tended to be in the inner-city schools which were, by most educational criteria, worse than other schools. Similarly they took pupils from the most disadvantaged homes. Thus any real effects of class size would be reduced in this sample. However, it must be noted that if class size were a powerful variable, there would still be a high loading on this factor.

2 In this sample of state schools the smallest classes still contained around 20 pupils. It could be argued that small class size is only important when small means four of five, as is the case with some of the leading public schools.

3 In this study only academic success was measured. No attempt was made to measure other variables which schools might consider to be important and in which class size might be influential.

In addition the important effect of the size of class on how the teacher felt was not investigated.

4 Nevertheless, despite these important caveats, this factor analysis makes it impossible to argue that class size, at least within the limits possible in current state schools, is a major influence in academic attainment at the primary school. This research is a clear instance of popular belief being overturned by evidence which is hard to refute.

CONCLUSIONS

I have taken three examples from medical, criminological and educational fields, in which factor analysis was employed in an attempt to answer broad questions concerning the relationships between highly important variables. In the medical instance the factor analysis revealed that long-term use of tranquillizers was associated with anxiety and that the users had few close friends and had been referred more often than controls to other agencies. All this suggests that anxious and lonely patients may go to their doctors for support and in so doing may receive tranquillizers thus confirming them as patients. Such analyses are frankly exploratory but they are suggestive of further clear research and in cases where clinical hypotheses are confirmed they can be highly valuable.

In the criminological field the results indicated that Q analysis could be valuable in the isolation of subgroups which again would have to be further studied. However, the Q analysis was valuable because the detection of such subgroups by other methods would be difficult, especially since cluster analyses are simply algorithms which are highly sample dependent.

In the educational field the results demonstrated with great clarity what variables were and were not associated with academic success at the primary school. The term 'associated with' has been chosen with care since it is dangerous to assume that there is a direct causal determination in such loadings, even though in some examples this may be the case.

From this discussion I hope a common theme has emerged. In these broad social science applications, the aim is to obtain a good measure of the variable in which we are interested (membership of a tranquillizer user group, membership of an offender group and academic success respectively) and to factor it alongside all possibly important variables of as wide a variety as possible. In almost all cases the relevant results will not provide definitive answers in themselves but will suggest clear hypotheses to test and will eliminate a large number of other possibilities. I should certainly like to see a wider use of this kind of exploratory factor analysis.

Chapter 10

Interpreting confirmatory and path analyses

In Chapter 6 confirmatory analysis and path analysis were discussed. It was shown there that confirmatory analysis is essentially a form of path analysis, although, as usually computed in the programs of Joreskog, it is path analysis of a particular kind.

Confirmatory analysis is usually used as more than a test of whether a particular factor analysis is a good solution, an aspect of the technique which is referred to as the measurement model. More often the structural model is invoked which examines relationships between the latent variables and which can put to the test complex psychological hypotheses.

In this chapter I shall deal only with the more simple examples since confirmatory analysis is best used after factor analysis has been well understood. In this chapter, therefore, I shall be content to give some indication of how these techniques can be used.

EXAMPLE 1: A CONFIRMATORY FACTOR ANALYTIC STUDY OF A TEST OF ORGANIZATIONAL REACTIONS BY GOFFIN AND JACKSON (1988)

Background and aim of the study

In this study Goffin and Jackson investigated both the primary factor structure of the index of organizational reactions (IOR), which claims to measure eight factors, and its secondary structure. The aim was to see whether eight factors was indeed the best account of the primary factor structure and to investigate its second-order structure. Second-order factors, as discussed in Chapter 5, are derived from the correlations between the primary factors, and this is an interesting aspect of this confirmatory analysis since in previous research the scales of the IOR were assumed to be orthogonal.

Subjects

A sample of 445 employees in a large financial institution were tested.

Test

The IOR, which uses 42 items to measure eight scales, was used. It might be pointed out that this is unlikely to be an effective test with so few items per factor, but see Kline (1992).

Factor analysis

Maximum likelihood confirmatory analysis, as computed in LISREL (see Chapter 6), was used to test a variety of models which included the following.

1 The null model which claims there are no factors in the inter-item correlations. This is only computed because two of the indices of fit – the parsimonious fit index and the delta index – use some of the information in the rejection of the null model.

Primary factor models

2 An eight factor orthogonal model in which factor loadings agree with the keyed scales. Thus if an item is keyed for scale 1 it is hypothesized to load on factor 1. These factors are, of course, uncorrelated.

3 A seven factor orthogonal model in which two scales (company identification and career future) are assumed, from previous research, to form one factor.

4 A seven factor orthogonal model in which the company identification factor and its items are excluded.

5 Three models identical to (2), (3) and (4) were also tried, except that their scales were allowed to be oblique.

Second-order models

These were used to examine further the oblique models should the above models fit. The following three models were tested:

1 a one factor model (two factors correlating 1);
2 a two factor orthogonal model;
3 a two factor oblique model in which the factors could be rotated to any position.

Comments

This confirmatory analysis is an example of the measurement model of the LISREL procedures. It is thus exactly equivalent to normal factor analysis. Indeed this examination of the structure of a test is identical to those examples cited in Chapter 8 in which simple structure factor analysis was used. Thus we could have rotated the inter-item correlation matrix to simple structure and examined the results. If, for example, the factors loaded the keyed items that would have confirmed the authors of the test. If the factors were oblique a second-order simple structure factor analysis could have been further rotated. Despite the statistical sophistication of the methods used by Goffin and Jackson (1988), the end result is unlikely to be much different from the simple structure approach.

Fit to model

As was pointed out in Chapter 6, a major difficulty with confirmatory analysis is the test of fit. In an attempt to deal with this Goffin and Jackson (1988) used six different indices:

1 the χ^2 goodness of fit;
2 the ratio of χ^2 to the degrees of freedom;
3 the delta index;
4 the parsimonious fit index (PFI);
5 the critical N;
6 the root mean square residual (RMR).

Comments on these indices

Goffin and Jackson (1988) openly discuss the many difficulties with these indices and I shall summarize their points. As was pointed out in Chapter 6 there are problems with the χ^2 test of significance especially in large samples where it is likely that the test will deem the fit unacceptable, even though the residual matrix is small. Thus in this instance this particular test of fit is best ignored.

It has been argued that the ratio of χ^2 to degrees of freedom overcomes this problem (test b, Table 10.1). A ratio of between 2 and 3 is said to be acceptable and the smaller the ratio the better the fit. Delta is an index which is independent of sample size. It runs from 0 to 1 and as a rule of thumb values of 0.9 and above indicate an acceptable fit. However, this index almost always selects as the best fit the model with the most free parameters, a rather important defect. This has been remedied with the PFI which penalized models with free parameters. However, it is not clear what values indicate an acceptable fit although the nearer 1 the better.

The critical N index is a formula which attempts to take into account the problems of the effects of sample size on χ^2. An N of around 200 suggests a fit and a value higher than this is satisfactory.

Finally the RMR which was mentioned in Chapter 6 was used. This is only suitable for judging between the fit of different models to the same data, but it has many of the problems associated with the delta index. The smaller the value the better the fit, but as with some of these other indices there are no cutoff points.

This discussion highlights the arguments in Chapter 6, namely that despite the attractions of confirmatory analysis there are such severe problems in testing the models that the practical power as distinct from the statistical elegance of the technique is unclear. None of these techniques is wholly reliable and phrases such as 'rule of thumb' and the lack of cutoff points indicate that these methods are not statistically rigorous.

To overcome these defects all these indices of fit were considered collectively with less attention paid to the weaker ones (χ^2, delta and RMR).

Results

Table 10.1 shows the fit indices of the various models.

Comments

The b versions of the models are those where the factors were allowed to be oblique. As was expected the null models were all

Table 10.1 Fit indices of first-order models

Model	χ^2	d.f.	χ^2/d.f.	Delta index	PFI	Critical N	RMR
Null42	11,516.16	903	12.75	0	0	38.55	0.316
Null37	9,740.42	703	13.86	0	0	35.90	0.307
I(a)	3,089.15	819	3.77	0.732	0.664	128.43	0.261
I(b)	1,783.23	791	2.25	0.845	0.740	214.49	0.051
II(a)	3,127.88	819	3.82	0.728	0.660	126.85	0.254
II(b)	2,066.25	798	2.58	0.821	0.725	185.85	0.055
III(a)	2,368.00	629	3.76	0.757	0.677	129.07	0.241
III(b)	1,434.73	608	2.36	0.853	0.737	207.25	0.052

Notes: d.f., degrees of freedom; Delta and PFI are fixed at zero in the case of null models.

rejected and clearly there are factors in this matrix. However, when it comes to selecting which is the best fit the difficulty with these indices becomes clear. The authors regard I(b) as the best fitting solution so it is instructive to examine the pattern of the fit indices.

First, all the orthogonal solutions appear to be worse fits than the oblique. Thus the ratios of χ^2 to degrees of freedom are all greater than 3 and the delta indices are all less than 0.9. However, this argument is not powerful since the same is true of the oblique solutions. The delta index would reject all models. The PFIs are higher for the oblique than the orthogonal solutions but with no cutoff points it is difficult to know how important this is. Furthermore, are the differences between the PFIs significant? Similarly the RMRs are lower for the oblique solutions and the critical Ns are higher. Generally then, all the evidence suggests that the oblique solutions are better than the orthogonal.

However, when it comes to choosing between the oblique models there has to be more subjective judgement. Thus the RMRs for all the oblique models are so similar that to choose between them would appear hazardous. The critical N favours I(b) but the PFIs are extremely close. The delta index rejects them all and the χ^2 ratio tests are highly similar. Although the I(b) solution has been chosen, careful examination of the evidence shows that it is little different in fit from the other solutions.

There is another perhaps more fundamental point. This model I(b) with eight oblique factors has been selected by these confirmatory tests although (despite the statistical claims of confirmatory analysis) the statistical differences in fit from the other solutions are dubious, and certainly small. However, this is but one model with a particular set of loadings. This model had items which loaded on only one factor and were zero on the others. In fact, in reality test items are quite different from this. Thus this model cannot reflect how the items actually load. Furthermore it is not impossible that with different loadings a seven factor model might have been a better fit.

In brief, as was pointed out in Chapter 6 a confirmatory study can only indicate that a model does or does not fit the data. It cannot confirm that this is the best fit from the infinity of possible models that might have been tried. Furthermore, as has been shown, the actual superiority of this I(b) model over the other oblique models is small. To argue from these results that I(b) is objectively better is not strictly permissible. However, it can be argued, on complex judgements concerning these fit indices, that I(b) is a better fit than the other solutions tried.

I shall not discuss the second-order analyses which used exactly the same procedures. A two factor oblique solution was chosen which is represented in Figure 10.1. This is a path diagram where the items loading the first-order factors and the second-order factors are shown.

However, in this second-order study the differences between the indices of fit for the one second-order solution and the oblique two factor solution are small. For example, the RMRs were 0.059 and 0.057, the delta indices were 0.836 and 0.839 and the PFIs were 0.725 and 0.727. I think one would have to argue that both these models fitted the data, given the nature of these indices.

Conclusions

This research by Goffin and Jackson (1988) is an excellent illustration of confirmatory analysis. It is confirmatory analysis in, to quote their terms, 'state of the art' form. It is also written with commendable clarity. Nevertheless, as has been made clear, the problems over the inefficiency of the indices of fit (in that they do not discriminate well between models and are affected by sample size and the freedom of parameters in the models) cannot be hidden. There is still a considerable subjective element in the selection of the best model. Furthermore, the fact that one particular model fits does not mean that other untried models would not also fit the result, so that unless the hypothesized model has a

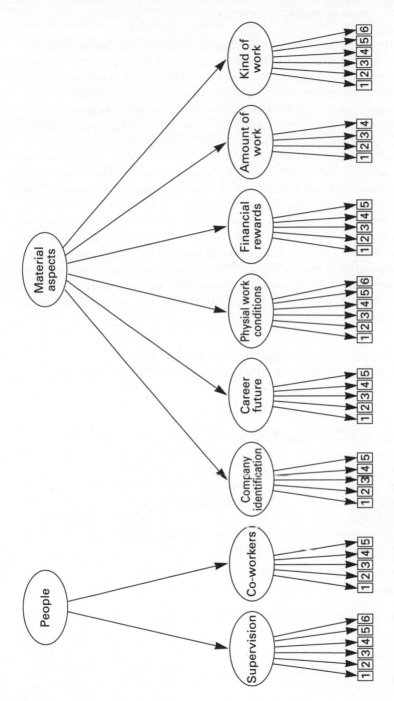

Figure 10.1 Path model of second-order factors

strong rational or empirical basis the interpretation has be cautious.

There is a further difficulty with the results. The authors have shown that an eight factor oblique model fits the inter-item correlations. However, the actual factor analysis of the items could never produce so perfect a simple structure. In addition these factors are loading on few items. As has been shown in Nunnally (1978) and Kline (1992), scales with so few items, if reliable, as these must be loading on a factor as they do, can hardly be valid. They must be, as was referred to in Chapter 8, bloated specifics. Thus despite the fact that the factor structure of the scales has been confirmed there is no evidence that the scales are valid.

Finally, it is useful to observe how this confirmatory analysis is easily represented in the path diagram of Figure 10.1. Notice that for simplicity the correlations between the factors, the curved arrows, have been left out. These would have to be included if, using path diagram rules rather than the maximum likelihood procedures of LISREL, one attempted to compute the path weights.

EXAMPLE 2: A STUDY OF THE LATENT STRUCTURE OF A SELF-MONITORING SCALE BY HOYLE AND LENNOX (1991)

Background and aim

This was a similar study to the first example in that it used confirmatory factor analysis in order to investigate the latent structure of a test of self-monitoring which was originally assumed to load a single factor. Recent studies had shown that the univariate model was unclear but had proposed a number of different factor structures so, in order to determine the best fitting model, Hoyle and Lennox (1991) tested five possible models using confirmatory analysis of two forms of the scale.

Sample

A sample of 1,113 college students was used.

Test

The self-monitoring scale (Snyder 1974) in 25 and 18 item forms was used.

Method

Five models derived from previous studies were tested using confirmatory analysis of the item correlations in the new sample. An exploratory factor analysis was also conducted but this will not be discussed here.

Figure 10.2 illustrates three primary factor models; two further second-order models are given in Figure 10.3. Model 1 in Figure 10.2 represents the unifactorial case with all items loading a single factor of self-monitoring. Model 2 shows the variance accounted for by three orthogonal factors, while model 3 is similar but the factors are correlated. Model 4 in Figure 10.3 represents a one factor second-order model while model 5 is an oblique two factor second-order model.

A few comments about these models are necessary because they illustrate an omnipresent danger with factor analysis, especially confirmatory analysis, namely that the elegance of the method becomes almost more important than the psychological hypotheses it was intended to test. For example, in all models except the unifactorial model extraversion is measured by five items. Given the broad nature of the extraversion variable, this is simply impossible, since even for a narrow factor a minimum of ten items is required to sample its universe of items, as Nunnally (1978) and Kline (1992) have demonstrated. If a factor fitted the model the only certain thing one might know about it was that it could not be extraversion.

Results

Model 3 is the most easy to fit of the first-order models since it is the least constrained. If this is rejected by implication the others must be also. In this investigation all these models were rejected. This being the case it was not strictly useful to test the higher-order models based on them but these were also rejected.

Because a more brief 18 item version is now used for this scale (although its psychometric efficiency must be even lower than the

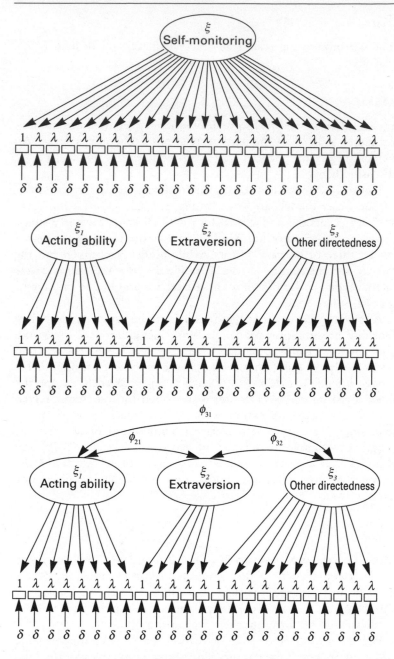

Figure 10.2 Three primary factor models

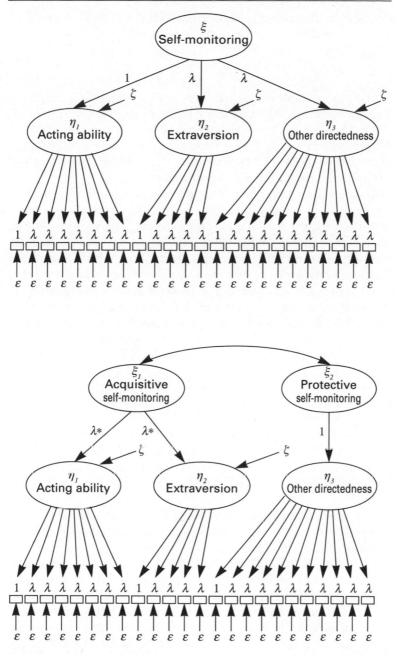

Figure 10.3 Two second-order models

original), all these models were tested with this version. Again they were all rejected.

Comments

I used this example of confirmatory analysis because it illustrates with great clarity a difficulty that has already been briefly discussed. Were these models rejected because the test is not good and no factorial model would fit the intercorrelations between the items, or were they rejected because with so large a sample the χ^2 test and any related indices of fit are almost bound to do so?

On general psychometric principles the self-monitoring scale is not promising. Twenty-five items are enough to sustain two scales and that with the barest minimum of items. Furthermore despite the large number of studies there is no clear evidence that the scale measures factors with external validity and which have been located in factor space. Thus it is quite possible that the models failed to fit because there is no real factorial structure to these items. Indeed it is striking that some of the most extensive studies used unrotated principal axes (see Chapters 3 and 4) to select items. The hopelessness of this procedure has been fully discussed in those chapters. I would guess that this scale is not a scale in any psychometric sense.

However, even if a structure were to be fitted, it must be noted that this is insufficient to demonstrate the validity of the test. Factor analysis, whether confirmatory or exploratory, indicates only that a factor or factors underlies the items. It does not show what those factors are. Thus even if these authors had been able to fit one of their models this would not have demonstrated the validity of the test. The factors would need identification and/or location in factor space.

One of the problems with confirmatory analysis with large samples concerns the χ^2 test. In example 1 the authors accepted that it would reject the model and used other indices. However, the other indices in this investigation of the self-monitoring scale also failed to reach significance. It is interesting to note that previous confirmatory studies of this scale claimed to be able to fit models (in one case 11 items and three factors and the mind boggles at the idiocy of such work – they must be specifics) but that examination of the results by Hoyle and Lennox (1991) showed again that the indices of fit rejected the models.

Conclusions

I believe that this study shows that the self-monitoring scale is not a valid test. The models do not fit and on psychometric grounds nobody would expect that they should. On the other hand the large samples and the problems with the indices of fit add some confusion to the issue.

Finally it should be noted that even if a model had been fitted the factors would have to be identified against external criteria or in factor space. Given the enormous computations involved in this work and the status of the test it is reasonable to consider whether a good simple structure factor analysis would not have answered their question just as well. Confirmatory analysis on a new sample might then have been in order if, and this is a big if, there had been any structure to confirm.

CONFIRMATORY ANALYSIS IN THE LIGHT OF THESE EXAMPLES

This book is intended to be an introduction to factor analysis and I have restricted my two examples of confirmatory analysis deliberately such that they were as analogous as possible to exploratory factor analyses. I hope that if these illustrative analyses can be understood then, as and when necessary, readers can dare further uncharted journeys into confirmatory analyses.

As was pointed out in the discussion of these examples it was the measurement model aspect of confirmatory analysis which was used rather than the structural model. However, it is structural modelling that is truly distinctive of confirmatory analysis and it is structural modelling which offers the greatest opportunities for the method. Here there can be no claim that exploratory analysis would be more simple and provide as useful information.

One of the most common applications of confirmatory analysis is in biometrics where for any variable, it could be an IQ score, a score on a particular personality test such as extraversion or even an item in a test, an investigation is made of the sources of variation: genetic factors, even divided up into dominant and additive factors, and environmental effects divided again into the shared and unshared effects.

Figure 10.4 sets out two different models which could be tested, one including biometric factors, the other psychosocial factors.

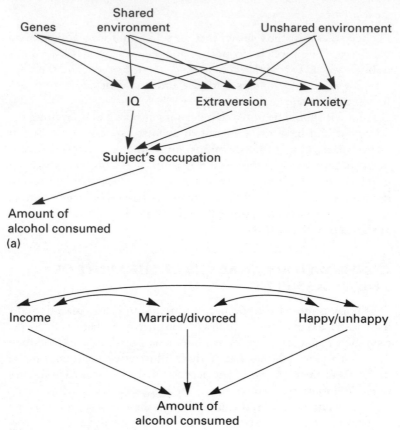

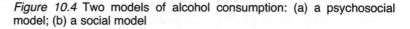

(b)

Figure 10.4 Two models of alcohol consumption: (a) a psychosocial model; (b) a social model

Using LISREL it is perfectly possible to compute the path coefficients, showing the degree of causality for the various paths shown. These diagrams are not, as is the case with all path diagrams, simple visual illustrations of hypotheses. Clearly testing two such different models would be highly valuable in the study of the determinants of excessive drinking.

Of course, obtaining the data to test the first model is more difficult than is the case for the second, but what is required is a sample of twins, identical and non-identical, some reared separately and some together. Other samples with subjects of differing degrees of relatedness can also be used. Then measures of extraversion, anxiety and intelligence would be administered together with an assessment of how much they drank. From the obtained correlations the partial regression coefficients for the paths could be estimated. The ability of the model to account for alcohol consumption is thus evaluated.

The second model is far simpler, involving no latent variables, and the estimation of the path coefficients makes for an easy comparison between the two. Of course if any of the variables in the first model turn out to be involved in drinking the adequacy of the second model even if there were some significant correlations is thrown into doubt.

As was shown from our examples in this chapter and the examples of path analysis in Chapter 6 the problem of adequate indices of fit means that model comparison and the decision whether to reject or accept is still highly subjective. In our first example, there was a subtle use of the whole range of indices, taking into account their known biasing factors and the nature of the sample. Nevertheless, there was considerable subjectivity in the conclusion that one model was better than another. Similarly this subjectivity of judgement was illustrated in the second study where the authors took a different view of two previous confirmatory analyses. The point here is that, despite the formidable statistical complexity of confirmatory analysis, in the end judgement is involved.

There is one further point about confirmatory analyses which must never be forgotten but often is amidst the algebra. Disregarding for the moment the problems of the indices of fit, if a model has been shown to fit it does not mean that this is the best model which fits the data. All it means is literally that it fits. If others have been rejected certainly these may be regarded as unsuitable but that a model fits does not imply that no others fit the data nor does it imply that the model is the best fit. It is essential to remember this when interpreting the results.

There is a final point which I should like to make. Mulaik (1987) argues that exploratory analysis can never answer definitively questions concerning the latent structure of a set of variables, claiming that factor analysis can only suggest structures and these require confirmation by confirmatory analysis.

First while it may be so for the statistician this is not the case for the social scientist who wishes to interpret any latent structure which emerges. Thus a great danger of confirmatory analysis is that it confirms a structure and regardless of what this is no further research is done. Suppose that, in example 2, model 3 had been accepted. As was argued a five item scale of extraversion could never be valid. The items must have been essentially tautologies or have been especially socially desirable. Thus the fact that a latent structure has been confirmed does not imply that the structure is what one was looking for or is of any psychological importance. As with all factors these must be identified not just from their loadings (merely face validity) but with reference to external criteria or location in factor space.

The second point concerns the status of exploratory factors. As has been discussed in our chapter on rotation, it has been shown by Cattell that rotation to simple structure can pick up real determiners of the matrix at least in artificial plasmodes. Furthermore he has shown that simple structure analyses are replicable. In any case since, as has been argued, it is necessary always to validate the identification of factors, whether their origin is exploratory or confirmatory is perhaps not important.

In brief, confirmatory analysis is a powerful technique. However, it must be used with proper understanding of its meaning and the problems of its indices of fit. Without this, delusion is all too possible.

Chapter 11

Summary and conclusions: the use and abuse of factor analysis in research

In the previous chapters I have examined and explicated the computations and nature of factor analysis. I have scrutinized different methods of condensation and discussed factor rotation. The problems of the indeterminacy of factor analysis, the infinity of mathematically equivalent solutions, the difficulties of replication and the need for simple structure have been described. All this led to a prescription for technically sound factor analyses, a prescription with which many psychometrists have essentially concurred. All this, of course, was factor analysis in the exploratory mode.

Confirmatory factor analyses, however, were also described together with the basic principles of path analysis. In the final section, as an aid to understanding the application of these techniques in various different aspects of psychology and the social sciences, examples of factor analyses were scrutinized and discussed in detail.

In this final chapter, in the light of all this discussion, I want to set out how factor analysis may be used to the best advantage in research in the social sciences. I shall discuss the kind of questions which it is ideally suited to answer and the problems which it can help to elucidate. I shall also indicate how it is possible to be misled by factor analysis and be carried away by the relative ease of factoring tests and measurements. Many results from factor analyses are essentially psychologically meaningless, artefacts of the algebraic constraints of the method, and all these problems, most of which have been discussed, will be brought into focus in this chapter. It is my hope that the abuse of factor analysis, its often pointless computation, can be thus stopped.

EXPLORATORY FACTOR ANALYSIS

To avoid repetition I shall assume that all studies are technically adequate and meet the most important points discussed in Chapter 5: a sufficiently large and representative sample of subjects; the right number of factors rotated to simple structure by adequate rotational procedures; a high ratio of subjects to variables. Any of these criteria will only be mentioned again when it is often neglected in the particular type of problem under discussion.

First, I shall list, with some comments, research problems and tasks for which factor analysis is particularly suited.

Investigating the structure of psychological tests, questionnaires or rating scales

It is important to know what factors account for the variance in any measure. If any sense is to be made of scores on a measure the variance should be largely attributable to one factor. Operationally each item in a test should load one factor significantly and no others. Thus exploratory factor analysis is ideal for demonstrating this structure.

However, in the factor analysis of tests and measures, as has been discussed in the chapters on factor analysis and in Chapter 8 where examples of this type of analysis were examined, there are a number of problems which can easily mislead the gullible user of factor analysis. Where problems have been discussed in earlier chapters they will be simply listed here. New points will be discussed.

1. The first unrotated component or factor is bound to be a general factor. Loadings on this cannot be taken as evidence, therefore, of a common factor running through the items. Factor rotation is essential.

2. Care should be taken in selecting the number of factors to rotate. Eigenvalues greater than 1 will give too many factors. It is sensible to try several methods if the indicators such as the Scree test and the MAP test do not agree.

3. Care should be shown with maximum likelihood factor analysis where the statistical test for the number of factors is affected by sample size.

4. Orthogonal (Varimax) and oblique (Direct Oblimin) rotation should both be tried. If the oblique is close to the orthogonal the

latter is useful because the pattern and structure loadings are the same.

5 The factor underlying a set of items should be replicated in a new sample.

6 It is not sufficient to show that a factor underlies a set of items.

7 This factor must be identified.

8 It is not sufficient to identify a factor through the content of the items loading on it, except in tests of attainment where the items are actual aspects of the knowledge required. Even in these cases further information is required.

9 Factors should be identified with reference to external criteria, e.g. correlations with other tests, correlations with occupational success or by locating the factor in factor space bounded by marker factors such as intelligence or extraversion. This is a specific method of test validation and is discussed in the next section.

10 Factors loading on only a few items (four or five) are almost certainly worthless. Reliable tests should have at least ten items. Factors with a few items are usually bloated specifics.

11 Care should be taken that factors are not simply tautologous, i.e. collections of items which are more or less paraphrases of each other.

12 A basic point needs to be stressed. There must be more subjects than items, preferably a high ratio so that a large N can be used, which is important to reduce the unreliability of the item inter-correlations as much as possible.

These points are all the commonplaces of test construction and have been fully discussed and scrutinized in *The Handbook of Psychological Testing* (Kline 1992). Nevertheless a surprisingly large number of tests are constructed and items loading a first unrotated factor are simply assumed to form a scale which is identified and regarded as valid on the basis of the item content. Tests which fail to meet these criteria of factor analytic test construction are valid only by luck.

Factor analysis and test validation

Factor analysis and test validation were discussed in Chapter 7 and were referred to briefly in the above section. My discussion here will be short.

Test validation is essentially an investigation or demonstration of what a test measures. Although it is, or should be, an intrinsic part of test construction, a large proportion of psychological tests are almost certainly not valid. One example was discussed in detail in Chapter 10. Almost all the studies of the self-monitoring scale showed that whatever it did measure was not unifactorial and hence was of little value for scientific measurement.

Two approaches are possible for the validation of tests. The first is to locate the factors in factor space. This entails factoring the test with the best known marker variables for ability, personality and interest. By rotating to simple structure it becomes obvious if the factors in question simply overlap established factors or are mixtures of them. If they are unitary, their position in factor space is useful in establishing what the test measures. Studies of this type were fully discussed in Chapter 7. All that I shall reiterate here is that having sufficient numbers in the sample and careful selection of the requisite numbers of factors is important.

A different method of using factor analysis in test validation is to investigate its factorial structure, as was discussed in the first section of this chapter, and then locate the emerging factors in factor space, as discussed above. This means that different factors may emerge from the test from those originally envisaged by the test authors. This method was exemplified in Chapter 7 by Kline and Cooper (1984a) in their study of the OATB. They found that ten factors emerged from the test, which were quite different from the ten scales actually scored in the OATB. Furthermore, one of these measured the obsessional or authoritarian personality factor. Again all the technical rules for adequate factor analyses should be observed.

Of course it must be stressed that factor analysis is not the only method of test validation. It is one aspect of establishing the construct validity of a test. Of extreme importance is the external, experimental validation of any factors emerging from the item correlations.

Factor analysis in the broad context

In Chapter 9 we showed how factor analysis could be used in the investigation of rather general wide ranging questions. We took examples from general medical practice (tranquillizer use), education (factors influencing educational progress) and criminology, where we examined a Q factor analysis. The principles underlying this approach can be simply stated. The variable of interest should be factored with all types of variable which could be held to influence it. Then all those variables, if any, which load a factor together with the target variable have by virtue of such loadings been shown to be relevant to it.

Some further examples will clarify the point.

What factors influence the outcome of psychotherapy?   One possible approach to answering this question is a factor analysis of the measures of outcome together with life events during the period of therapy; measures of the patient–therapist interaction; type of therapy given; length of therapy; diagnostic category; age of patient; sex of patient; age of therapist; sex of therapist.

If measures of outcome loaded on a factor together with certain life events, e.g. forming a successful relationship, and this had the highest loading, this would be extremely interesting. If the type of therapy had no loading, again this would be of importance. Similarly if there were different patterns of loadings for males and females this too would be relevant. If none of these variables loaded the outcome factor, then clinical psychology would have to think again.

This is not intended to be a full list of variables that might or should be included in such an investigation. Nor is it argued that such a study would necessarily yield an answer to this question. However, it is argued that such a study could well yield important information and deserves to be tried.

What factors influence divorce?   Here we would have to be careful in our sampling of subjects. For example, it could well be the case that in bad marriages the longer the marriage continues the worse it gets, until ended by divorce. However, length of marriage could not go into a factor analysis of a sample of individuals since the better marriages last longer, by definition. Thus we would have to sample individuals 10 years after marriage, and other samples would be similarly homogeneous for age. It might also be sensible to have single sex samples.

Among the variables to be included would be personality and ability variables, since it is possible that anxious individuals, for example, who are also extravert might be more difficult to live with than some other configurations of personality. Income, outgoings, number of children, sexual satisfaction, whether desire for children was met, whether partner was away for long periods (e.g. army personnel), illnesses, religious beliefs, size of house relative to family size, all might usefully be included. No doubt readers can think of many more relevant variables which should be put into the factor analysis.

Of course differences in variables between partners might be important and these should be included in the analyses, e.g. difference in intelligence, difference in extraversion. Such variables would go a long way to answering questions as to whether similarities or differences lead to better marriages, whether this is irrelevant or whether it depends upon which variables are similar or different.

A simple structure rotation of these variables with the dummy variable of divorced or married might well throw up some important determinants of divorce. Of course we would not expect variables to load very highly on the divorce factor. Rather we might expect a number of variables to load moderately and significantly since it is likely that divorce is multi-determined.

It should be noted that this design allows for historical hypotheses to be examined in that the marital status of parents and siblings and other relatives could be included. Of course if adopted children and siblings reared apart were used some genetic hypotheses might be tested, although for this the structural model of confirmatory analysis is more suited than relatively simple exploratory factor analysis.

These two illustrations, together with the three published examples of this application of factor analysis in Chapter 9, are sufficient to see the power of this technique to answer difficult and wide-ranging questions. Often the results will be far from definitive. However, they will always highlight variables which deserve study by other methods. Thus if differing religion among partners, for example, proved related to divorce it would make sense to carry out some more intensive investigation of this variable. In addition such studies often demonstrate clearly that variables which one might have thought, *a priori*, were important in the determination of some behaviour were simply irrelevant to it, i.e. they did not load on the relevant factor. This is important since it means that the theory which postulated their relevance can be abandoned.

So far in this chapter we have summarized what has been argued throughout this book, namely that technically adequate factor analyses are able to answer with some precision questions concerning the validity of tests, indicating clearly what they do and do not measure. It must be pointed out at this juncture that such minute examination of the structure of tests by factor analysis and the elucidation of their factors are not just academic exercises for factor analysts. Precise measurement is essential for all scientific endeavour and one of the problems of psychology is that there are huge numbers of tests, of which the majority are not valid. Research with invalid tests is worse than useless: it can be actually misleading.

In addition factor analyses are able to untangle a variety of questions in highly complex multidetermined contexts, as our examples illustrate. Even though they may not be able to provide definitive answers to such problems they are valuable in ruling out lines of enquiry and in suggesting variables that should be scrutinized in further studies with more detail.

Nunnally (1978), in the excellent book to which I have frequently referred, discusses what he calls a variety of ways to fool yourself with factor analysis. Some of these points are so important that although they have been discussed as we dealt with the issues in the relevant chapters they should be emphasized in this concluding chapter. This is because they are not simply academic points made by fussy statisticians. On the contrary, they lead to false conclusions. Furthermore they are not rare. Indeed, as Cattell (1978) pointed out, in the field of personality measurement many of the disparate findings were the result of just such mistakes.

However, it should not be thought that researchers fool themselves simply because they ignore the technical criteria for adequate factor analyses, which have been discussed throughout this book, although this is sometimes the cause of the error. In addition there are errors of interpretation and implication.

THE ERRORS OF FACTOR ANALYSIS

Interpreting the first principal component or factor

As we saw from the computations of Chapter 3, the first principal component is always a general factor. Thus to interpret this as evidence for a general factor is not admissible. Similarly the argument that there is one large factor in the matrix, based on the unrotated factors, is not viable. The only interest in the unrotated matrix is to be able to say that there are *x* significant components or factors accounting for the correlations. The number of factors, as distinct from their loadings, will remain constant.

Using too small samples

As was clear from the computations of factor analysis, the aim is to account for the correlations of the variables. The smaller the sample the larger the standard error of the correlations and thus the more error is contained in the factor analysis. Samples of less than 100 could produce misleading results. In factor analysis the larger the sample the better.

Too stringent or too lax a view of what constitutes a salient loading

As was made clear, what constitutes a salient loading on a factor is to an extent arbitrary. To insist that all loadings are greater than 0.8 (as is done in some studies of artificial matrices) is quite unrealistic and misleading since a loading of 0.7, for example, means that virtually 50 per cent of that variable's variance is explained by the factor. Generally a sensible guideline seems to be to accept 0.3 as a salient loading. Some eminent researchers, including Cattell, when they use large samples drop below this figure and may use small loadings, e.g. 0.19, if these are significant (despite the problems of computing significance). However, I believe that even if such coefficients are statistically significant it is misleading to regard them as salient loadings simply because they account for so little of the variance. Indeed, given the errors of measurement in psychological variables it is more sensible to regard them as trivial. Certainly this difficulty seems to have plagued the development of some of Cattell's tests.

Taking the criterion for the number of factors too literally

It is essential that the correct number of factors be rotated, as has been shown. However, apart from the statistical method of maximum likelihood factor analysis, the procedures are arbitrary although some have more convincing rationales or demonstrations of efficiency than do others. If good methods such as the MAP and the Scree tests disagree both numbers should be rotated and the best solution needs to be decided on other grounds. Finally, as has been mentioned, in maximum likelihood factor analysis there are statistical tests for the number of factors. However, large samples are needed for accurate maximum likelihood factoring and in such samples the numbers of factors selected are trivially different from those of the algorithms.

Factors should be replicated

If working in a fresh field where the number and nature of the factors is unknown factors should be replicated in new samples. Only replicated factors should be interpreted.

There are various indices for matching factors but by replication I mean something less rigorous than statistical matching, namely that the subjective interpretation of the factors would be the same. This would be indicated by the fact that the same variables would have salient loadings on the factors. If this is the case one can have some confidence in them.

Interpreting factors from their factor loadings

In test construction this is one of the easiest roads to delusion. The interpretation of factors from item content is not evidence of validity. In fact this is simply face validity, claiming that a test measures something from its appearance. It is always essential to validate any factors either with reference to external criteria or by locating them in factor space. This cannot be stressed too much. All the established marker factors in the fields of ability and personality have been identified in this way. Their validity is not attested only by item content.

There is no mystery in insisting that factors be thus identified. A factor could load on items which were paraphrases, or had a particular format. It would thus be a specific. A factor might load items which attracted socially desirable responses or acquiescent responses and such a factor would be a measure only of these response sets.

Indeed the failure to identify a factor other than by its loadings is about the most common form of misleading factor analytic research.

Factor pattern, structure and reference structure

As was made clear in Chapter 5, in orthogonal rotations factor pattern and structure are the same. Thus there is no problem of interpretation. The factor loadings may be regarded as correlations and the factors interpreted accordingly.

However, this is not the case in oblique rotations. Here often the factor structure refers to the reference structure while the pattern contains the partial regression weights. The pattern is frequently interpreted as if these loadings are correlations, which is not strictly the case although their size clearly indicates their importance. In some instances, as Nunnally argues, the reference vector factors (orthogonal to the oblique factors running through clusters of variables) can be very different from those factors when the factors are highly correlated, although reference vector loadings are related to factor loadings. This is the reason why Nunnally so strongly objects to them. What is important is that it is sensible to be clear which matrix is being interpreted. It is wrong to interpret the oblique pattern as if it were a structure matrix.

Failure to obtain simple structure

As was argued in Chapter 5, rotation to simple structure usually yields replicable factors and the technical rules for reaching simple structure have been explicated. In exploratory factor analysis simple structure and factor replicability is the answer to the problem of the indeterminacy of factor analysis. An infinity of solutions there may be, but the simple structure solution is best. Certainly, as Cattell (1978) has demonstrated, failure to reach simple structure is the main cause of discrepant results in the field of personality testing. Thus it is essential to reach simple structure, and this can easily be done by following the technical rules for adequate factor analyses.

These are the main causes of confusion and misleading results in exploratory analyses. However, as we have seen in Chapters 6 and 10, some psychologists regard exploratory analysis as old hat, arguing that many of its problems can be overcome by confirmatory analysis. We shall now, to conclude this chapter, and indeed the book, summarize the uses and abuses of confirmatory factor analysis. Since this book is essentially about factor analysis I shall be concerned almost exclusively with the measurement rather than the structural model.

USES OF CONFIRMATORY ANALYSIS

Confirmatory analysis is used to test hypotheses. Thus in the examples which were discussed in Chapter 10, hypotheses derived from previous studies with the measures under examination were tested. Of course, in other circumstances hypotheses concerning the factor loadings can be derived from psychological theories. Once specified the models can be put to the test. Mulaik (1987) has even suggested that all exploratory analyses should be completed by a confirmatory analysis.

In principle this seems like an excellent procedure. An objection to exploratory analysis is always that it is exploratory whereas science normally proceeds by hypothesis testing. Furthermore confirmatory analysis is not simply an algorithm but has a statistical basis. These arguments are, in principle, sound, although as has been pointed out, simple structure factor analysis can be used to test hypotheses. Thus if a factor is hypothesized with loadings on certain variables and this appears in a simple structure analysis, it is reasonable to argue that the hypothesis has not been refuted and that in the opposing case it has been refuted.

PROBLEMS WITH CONFIRMATORY FACTOR ANALYSIS

However, these great advantages of statistical hypothesis testing are, as was seen in the examples of Chapter 10, considerably lessened by the fact that the original χ^2 test is far too sensitive with large samples so that quite good fits are rejected. With small samples, on the other hand, the χ^2 test may have difficulty in selecting between different models and can accept as fitting quite discrepant models.

Of course, as was seen in Chapter 10, other indices of fit have been developed but these are not without problems and a degree of subjectivity enters into their use. Confirmatory analysis is not as statistically powerful as it first appears.

However, there is also a conceptual problem with confirmatory analysis which can lead researchers into difficulties. The fact that a model is confirmed, quite apart from the statistical problems with the indices of fit, means only that this particular model fits the data. It does not mean that other models might not fit and fit better. Since the infinity of models cannot be tested, unless the model has a sound rationale, the procedure is again less powerful than it seems.

Finally there is a further problem of how precisely the model is specified. If only a few loadings are specified it is obviously easier to fit this model than one with precise specifications. However, the value of a loosely specified model is small. Again much depends upon the provenance of the model.

From this it is clear that confirmatory analysis can be valuable in confirming hypotheses but much depends on the sample size, the indices of model fit, the rationale and provenance of the model and the availability of competing models which have not been put to the test. With careful consideration of all these problems, confirmatory analysis is a useful technique. However, interpretations which have not taken these into account can be misleading in the extreme.

FINAL COMMENTS

In brief, it is clear that factor analysis, both exploratory and confirmatory, can be a valuable research method for a variety of questions in the social sciences. However, it must be properly used, having regard to all the problems and difficulties which can render the results misleading and of little scientific value. This can only be done with an understanding of how factor analyses are computed. Without this understanding factor analysis leads to a numerical psychobabble all too common in the social sciences.

References

Adorno, T.W., Frenkel-Brunswick, E., Levinson, D.J. and Sanford, R.N. (1950) *The Authoritarian Personality*. New York: Harper.

Arrindel, W.A. and Ende, van der J. (1985) 'An empirical test of the utility of the observations-to-variables-ratio in factor and components analysis', *Applied Psychological Measurement* 9: 165–78.

Barrett, P. and Kline, P. (1982) 'An item and radial parcel factor analysis of the 16PF Questionnaire', *Personality and Individual Differences* 3: 259–70.

Carroll, J.B. (1983) 'Studying individual differences in cognitive abilities: implications for cross-cultural studies', in S.H. Irvine and J.W. Berry (eds) *Human Assessment and Cultural Factors*. New York: Plenum, pp. 213–35.

Cattell, R.B. (1971) *Abilities Their Structure Growth and Action*. New York: Houghton Mifflin.

—— (1978) *The Scientific Use of Factor Analysis*. New York: Plenum.

Cattell, R.B. and Kline, P. (1977) *The Scientific Study of Personality and Motivation*. London: Academic Press.

Cattell, R.B. and Schuerger, J.M. (1978) *Personality Theory in Action*. Champaign: IPAT.

Child, D. (1990) *The Essentials of Factor Analysis*. London: Cassell.

Comrey, A.L. (1962) 'The minimum residual method of factor analysis', *Psychological Reports* 11: 15–18.

Digman, J.N. (1990) 'Personality structure: emergence of the five factor model', *Annual Review of Psychology* 14: 417–40.

Goffin, R.D. and Jackson, D.N. (1988) 'The structural validity of the Index of Organizational Reactions', *Multivariate Behavioural Research* 23: 327–47.

Goldberg, D. (1978) *General Health Questionnaire*. Windsor: NFER.

Gorsuch, R.L. (1983) *Factor Analysis*, 2nd edn. Hillsdale: Erlbaum.

Guilford, J.P. (1956) *Psychometric Methods*. New York: McGraw-Hill.

—— (1967) *The Nature of Human Intelligence*. New York: McGraw-Hill.

Hakstian, A.R. (1971) 'A comparative evaluation of several prominent factor tranformation methods', *Psychometrika* 36: 175–93.

Hampson, S. (1975) 'The personality characteristics of certain groups of mentally abnormal offenders', PhD thesis, University of Exeter.

Hampson, S. and Kline, P. (1977) 'Personality dimensions differentiating certain groups of abnormal offenders from non-offenders', *British Journal of Criminology* 17: 310–31.

Harman, H.H. (1976) *Modern Factor Analysis*, 3rd edn. Chicago: University of Chicago Press.

Hashemi, P.T. (1981) 'The factor structure of the Eysenck Personality Questionnaire and the 16 Personality Factor Questionnaire', PhD thesis, University of Exeter.

Heim, A.W. (1975) *Psychological Testing* London: Oxford University Press.

HMSO (1967) *Children and their Primary Schools. Volume 2: Research and Surveys.* London: HMSO.

Holley, J.W. and Guilford, J.P. (1964) 'A note on the G index of agreement', *Educational and Psychological Measurement* 24: 749–53.

Horn, J. and Knapp, J.R. (1973) 'On the subjective character of the empirical base of Guilford's Structure of Intellect Model', *Psychological Bulletin* 80: 33–43.

Hotelling, H. (1933) 'Analysis of a complex of statistical variables into principal components', *Journal of Educational Psychology* 24: 417–41.

Hoyle, R.H. and Lennox, R.D. (1991) 'Latent structure of self-monitoring', *Multivariate Behavioural Research* 26: 511–40.

Joreskog, K.G. (1973) 'General methods for estimating a linear structure equation system', in A.S. Goldberger and O.D. Duncan (eds) *Structural Equation Models in the Social Sciences.* New York: Seminar Press.

Joreskog, K.G. and Sorbom, D. (1984) *LISREL V1: User's Guide*, 3rd edn. Mooresville: Scientific Software.

Kaiser, H.F. (1958) 'The varimax criterion for analytic rotation in factor analysis', *Psychometrika* 23: 187–200.

Kline, P. (1991) *Intelligence: The Psychometric View.* London: Routledge.

—— (1992) *The Handbook of Psychological Testing.* London: Routledge.

—— (1993) *Personality: The Psychometric View.* London: Routledge.

Kline, P. and Barrett, P. (1983) 'The factors in personality questionnaires among normal subjects', *Advances in Behaviour Research and Therapy* 5: 141–202.

Kline, P. and Cooper, C. (1984a) 'A construct validation of the Objective Analytic Test Battery (OATB)', *Personality and Individual Differences* 5: 323–38.

—— and —— (1984b) 'A factorial analysis of the authoritarian personality', *British Journal of Psychology* 75: 171–6.

Kline, P. and Lapham, S. (1991) 'The validity of the PPQ: A study of its factor structure and its relationship to the EPQ', *Personality and Individual Differences* 12: 631–5.

Kline, P., Auld, F. and Cooper, C. (1987) 'Five new personality scales: their loaction in the factor space of personality measures', *Journal of Clinical Psychology* 43: 328–36.

Loehlin, J.C. (1987) *Latent Variable Models.* Hillsdale: Erlbaum.

May, J. and Kline, P. (1987) 'Extraversion, neuroticism, obsessionality and the Type A behaviour pattern', *British Journal of Medical Psychology* 60: 253–9.

Mulaik, S.A. (1972) *The Foundations of Factor Analysis*. New York: McGraw-Hill.

—— (1987) 'A brief history of the philosohical foundations of exploratory factor analysis', *Multivariate Behavioural Research* 22: 267–305.

Nunnally, J. (1978) *Psychometric Theory*. New York: McGraw-Hill.

Parker, C. and Kline, P. (1993) 'Personality, interest and occupational choice', in preparation.

Paykel, E.S. and Mangen, S.P. (1980) *Interview for Recent Life Events*, Department of Psychiatry, St George's Hospital Medical School.

Pickering, P.M. (1986) 'Psychosocial characteristics of long-term tranquilliser users', PhD thesis, Department of Psychology, University of Exeter.

Popper, K. (1959) *The Logic of Scientific Discovery*. New York: Basic Books.

Royce, J.R. (1963) 'Factors as theoretical constructs', in D.N. Jackson and S. Messick (eds) *Problems in Human Assessment*. New York: McGraw-Hill.

Snyder, M. (1974) 'Self-monitoring of expressive behaviour', *Journal of Personality and Social Psychology* 30: 526–37.

Spearman, C. (1904) 'General intelligence: objectively determined and measured', *American Journal of Psychology* 15: 201–92.

Thomson, G.H. (1954) *The Geometry of Mental Measurement*. London: University of London Press.

Thurstone, L.L. (1947) *Multiple Factor Analysis: A Development and Expansion of Vectors of the Mind*. Chicago: University of Chicago Press.

Velicer, W.F. (1976) 'Determining the number of components from the matrix of partial correlations', *Psychometrika* 41: 321–7.

Name index

Subject index

ability 4, 6, 7, 8, 9, 12, 13, 34, 63, 66, 77, 114–15, 121, 123, 126, 140; psychology of 9
academic success: study of 152–6
Ai3Q test: use of 104, 107, 109, 110, 111
attainment 4, 8, 9, 175
Auld picture preference test (PPT) 114, 116, 117, 118–20
authoritarian personality: measurement of 102–8

beta weights 38, 41, 85, 86
Binormamin rotation 68
biometrics 169
Biquartmin rotation 68
bloated specifics 12, 112, 113, 140, 164, 175; and test construction 128–9

Cattell 16PF personality test 104, 106, 115, 117, 121, 138, 139, 141, 142, 146
characteristic equation 29
characteristic roots 29, 30, 32
characteristic vectors 29, 30, 32
communality 43, 44, 47, 48, 49, 50, 53, 54, 67, 74; and iterative computation of 45–6; and squared multiple correlation (SMC) 46
components 35; and factors 36–9, 44–5
comprehensive ability battery

(CAB) 115, 116, 121
computers: use of 1, 28–9, 30, 49, 50, 57, 62, 63–4, 67, 69, 71, 75, 80, 87, 89, 90, 93, 96, 124; *see also* LISREL
condensation 40, 43–55; *see also* factor analysis, principal components analysis
confirmatory factor analysis 80–99, 105, 126, 130, 139, 178, 182; examples of 157–72; interpretation of 157–72; maximum likelihood 158; problems of 11, 183–4; use of 183–4
convergence 32
correlation 22, 28, 36, 40, 44, 56, 175; coefficient 3–4, 126, 147; definition of 18–21; error 42; inter-item 164; item 126, 165; multiple 26–7, 38; Pearson product-moment 18–19, 126, 130; replication of 22; reproduction of 39–40; and rotation 61–2, 63; and scatter diagrams 23–5; semipartial 26; squared multiple (SMC) 46, 51, 54
correlation matrix 4–5, 7, 22, 29, 30, 32, 36, 37, 38, 39, 40, 43, 44, 46, 47, 53, 54, 64, 68, 92, 93; inter-item 159; population 49; and principal factor analysis 45; tetrachoric 126